MW01028824

Incredible Metal Detecting Discoveries

True Stories of Amazing Treasures Found by Everyday People

By Mark Smith   .

Incredible Metal Detecting Discoveries

ISBN-13: 978-1499504019
ISBN-10: 1499504012
Incredible Metal Detecting Discoveries: True Stories of Amazing Treasures Found by Everyday People

Copyright 2014 and Beyond All Rights Reserved
Mark Smith

No part of this book may be reproduced, copied, or transmitted in any form without the written consent of the author.

Table of Contents

Introduction

My name is Mark Smith, and I am addicted to finding treasure with my metal detector. It's the truth, and I will happily admit it, but the funny thing is this. I am not alone with my rather healthy addiction. There are countless other men and women all over our great blue planet who have also been bitten by the treasure hunting bug. Once it sinks its teeth in, there is no turning back.

We eagerly comb the globe looking for our next fix. It could be a piece of gold jewelry encrusted with diamonds. It could be an old coin from the Roman Empire, or it could be a long lost relic that has been buried for hundreds of years.

Introduction

We are all helplessly and hopelessly addicted. You can see it in our eyes. There is a wild untamed fire burning deep within. A desire to explore, to find and most importantly a desire to recover. Okay, maybe I went too far with the whole "untamed fire burning deep within" part, but you get the idea.

It is all about the thrill of the hunt and the idea that you could very well be unearthing an amazing piece of treasure that has been hidden from sight for who knows how long. I am getting excited just thinking about it. It really gets my blood pumping.

If you happen to be a treasure hunting addict like myself, then you already know just how exciting it can be digging up some long lost piece of treasure. There is nothing quite like it. The glimmer of a gold ring in the bottom of a beach scoop. The weight of an old copper, bronze, silver or gold coin in the palm of your hand. It is fascinating, fun and highly addictive.

I often find myself looking at the treasures I have recovered over the years and thinking to myself, "I can't believe I found this stuff with my metal detector." I know I am not alone either. I have met quite a few great people who do the same exact thing.

All of us cherish our finds no matter how simple they may be. We get to hold a physical piece of fascinating history in

Introduction

the palm of our hands. What other hobby gives a person this opportunity? None that I know of.

There are incredible untold stories just waiting below the surface of the earth and all it takes is a metal detector to locate them. What follows next just so happens to be some of the most incredible metal detecting stories in the world. If you are not already hooked on the idea of metal detecting, I can guarantee you will be once you are done reading these stories. Every single one of them is true. This is the reality of metal detecting. Jump right in. Dig in and prepare to be amazed!

Incredible Gold Finds

Gold is one thing that every single person swinging a metal detector wants to find and there are plenty of people finding it too. Gold has a way of doing strange things to a person. Finding gold can create an itch that you can never seem to scratch. Finding one piece of that funny yellow metal only fuels your desire to recover more and more.

Some people may get a mild case of gold fever, while others get consumed by the concept of uncovering some long lost gold treasure that could be worth millions of dollars. Either way, searching for gold with a metal detector is a truly great experience, especially when you do get to see that glint of yellow.

It doesn't matter if you are a hardcore beach hunter, or a dedicated nugget shooter. Seeing a piece of gold in the bottom of a scoop or encrusted in earth will quicken your pulse, make your mind race and possibly even make you jump for joy.

If you have been lucky enough to find some gold, then you know exactly what I am talking about. If you are still looking for your first piece of gold, then these stories will inspire you to get out there and claim your own share. We can all learn a thing or two about these incredible metal detecting finds. Dig in!

The Mojave Nugget

People have been heading to the west coast of the United States in pursuit of gold since it was first discovered there in the early 1800s. The Gold Rush created an almost mass hysteria in the area as people fought tooth and nail to claim their stake.

They worked hard to recover gold. The tools of the trade were rock hammers, chisels, pick axes, gold pans and sluices made from wood and metal. They didn't have the modern conveniences of using something like a metal detector to help them locate the mother lode.

The Mojave Nugget

California has always been and still is to this day an excellent place to locate gold. Using a metal detector makes the process a little easier, but in order to get to those good gold bearing fields you will have to travel to some pretty harsh environments like the Mojave Desert in the Southwestern United States.

It is here that the temperatures during the day can get hot enough to fry an egg on a slab of rock. You would think the setting sun would be welcomed with open arms, but when that bright orange ball in the sky slowly creeps below the horizon, the temperatures can plummet fast enough to chill your favorite beverage.

If these harsh conditions are not enough to make you want to stay in the comfort of your modern home, then just think of the creatures that call the Mojave Desert home. Deadly scorpions and rattlesnakes as fat as your thigh not only like these conditions, they thrive in them, but these things don't even enter the mind of a person who has a bad case of gold fever. Their mind is on the find. They are looking for that magical yellow metal, and that is exactly what Ty Paulsen found way back in 1977 with his metal detector.

Feast your eyes on the largest gold nugget recovered in the state of California with a metal detector, The Mojave Nugget.

The Mojave Nugget

Could you imagine finding this monster gold nugget with a metal detector? It would be like finding the tip of an iceberg, and it would just keep getting bigger as you slowly or frantically removed rocks and desert sand from around it. If it was me, I would most likely need a to change my pants after unearthing a gold nugget of this magnitude.

How Much Does This Monster Nugget Weigh?
It can be difficult to determine the size of something like this when you are just staring and drooling over a picture.

The Mojave Nugget

This is a big one. It weighs 156 troy ounces. That equals 4.9 kilograms or a massive 10 pounds 11 ounces. I still have a hard time wrapping my head around the size of this nugget. It is huge, and I promise you there are some that are even bigger!

Where Was the Mojave Nugget Unearthed?
That is the million dollar question isn't it? The exact location of this monster nugget find is still not known. It was recovered somewhere very close to the city of Randsburg, California in an area where gold has been known to exist in large volumes. There are plenty of mines in the area, but the exact location where this beauty was unearthed still remains behind tight lips. Who could blame them? Would you be willing to tell anyone the exact location if you discovered this giant nugget? I don't think I would.

There are also quite a few interesting stories floating around out there about how this nugget was found. Ty was using a metal detector when he located it. That part we know, but the exact kind or model of metal detector he was using is still up for debate.

Some people are saying it was a metal detector that was designed to locate landmines and others are saying that Ty had several coils attached to his vehicle. He would just drive very slowly through the desert until his coils alerted him to the treasure below. We may never know because Ty Paulsen has since departed the land of the living.

The Mojave Nugget

What Happened to the Mojave Nugget?

Ty sold his amazing find to a private collector by the name of Robert E. Peterson. Don't worry, this massive gold nugget did not stay hidden behind closed doors in a private collection.

Margie and Robert E. Peterson decided to donate their rather impressive gold nugget collection to the Natural History Museum of Los Angeles County. The entire collection of gold nuggets consists of over 130 pieces of gold that total more than 1660 troy ounces. That is just over 113 pounds or 51 kilograms of pure golden delight. Sitting at the middle of the collection is the Mojave Gold Nugget. As of this writing, this is the biggest gold nugget that has been recovered in California soil with a metal detector.

If you are planning a trip to the area, I strongly suggest you visit this exhibit. Once you see the Mojave Nugget, the cleaning crew at the museum will need to come along and pick your jaw up off the floor.

Museum Contact Information

It is always a good idea to call ahead to make sure this exhibit is still on display.
Museum website: http://www.nhm.org/
Phone number: 213-763-3466
email: info@nhm.org

The Boot of Cortez

This next story will lay the theory "an expensive metal detector is the best metal detector" to rest. I mentioned in my book entitled: "Metal Detecting: A Beginner's Guide to Mastering the Greatest Hobby In the World," knowing how to use your metal detector properly is much more important than buying a metal detector with an expensive price tag. This story drives this fact straight home and proves that sometimes simple is so much better.

Once again we have to travel to that harsh desert landscape for this incredible story. This one takes place just south of the United States border in the Sonoran Desert where the daytime temperatures can exceed 125 degrees Fahrenheit (51 degrees Celsius). It is said that the wind here is so ferocious that its hot breath literally strips the water from any living creature in a matter of minutes. This area is not exactly a walk through the park with your metal detector. You have to be conditioned to handle this type of environment, and you have to be a hardcore treasure hunter to spend any extended amount of time here.

This area of desert may seem harsh and devoid of life, but it is rich in treasure folklore. There are countless legends of mountains of gold and silver just waiting for the would be treasure hunter to uncover. These legends are attractive to anyone who has been bitten by the treasure hunting bug.

The Boot of Cortez

Could you imagine discovering a mountain of gold? What would it be like to walk into some long lost desert cave where the walls were lined with the richest gold veins the world has ever seen? Are you ready to take your metal detector out to the desert yet? I know I am. If you are not, then you will be by the time you are done reading this story.

The Sonoran Desert is no stranger to gold. There are numerous gold and silver mines throughout the Sonoran Desert region, and in 1989 history was made by a local Mexican prospector in a canyon close to the Gran Desierto de Altar.

This local prospector whose name seems to be magically erased from the history books found the largest gold nugget in the entire western hemisphere with a metal detector. If you thought the Mojave Nugget was incredible, you haven't seen anything yet.

Instead of sweating his life away prospecting for gold the old fashioned way, this prospector decided to put technology to work for him. He purchased an inexpensive metal detector from Radio Shack. The exact model he used is not known, but given the era of the find and the fact that he purchased this metal detector at Radio Shack means one thing. He was using an entry level machine without any fancy bells and whistles.

Did this prospector randomly pick an area and blindly

search it with his entry level metal detector?
No he didn't. He carefully picked an area in a canyon
where large gold nuggets have been found in the past.

Once he decided on this area, he slowly and very
methodically combed every single inch of desert sand
using a tight grid like pattern. Hunting in a grid pattern is
essential if you want to leave nothing behind but
footprints. I cover this metal detecting technique in great
detail in my book entitled: "Metal Detecting: A Beginner's
Guide to Mastering the Greatest Hobby In the World."

Was This Method an Instant Success?
No it was not. This prospector faced what many of us face
when using our metal detectors on a regular basis. He
uncovered quite a bit of trash before he finally hit the
mother lode.

He spent about two weeks digging scrap iron targets and
old bullets in this harsh desert environment, but his hard
work and dedication was about to pay off more than he
could have ever imagined

His entry level metal detector alerts him to a rather large
target in the sand. This target is so big that it must be an
old iron chunk of trash, but this prospector ignores this
idea and gets down on his hands and knees to uncover his
find.

At first it appears to be a good sized nugget laying in the

ground, but as he continues to move the sand and rock away, the nugget grows in size. By the time he is done, he has unearthed a nugget that measures 10.75 inches in height (27.3 centimeters) and 7.25 inches wide (18.41 centimeters).

This monster nugget weighs in at 389.4 troy ounces. That is 26 pounds, 10 ounces (12 kilograms) worth of almost pure gold. Not only is the nugget huge, but it is oddly shaped just like a boot. Hence the name, "The Boot of Cortez."

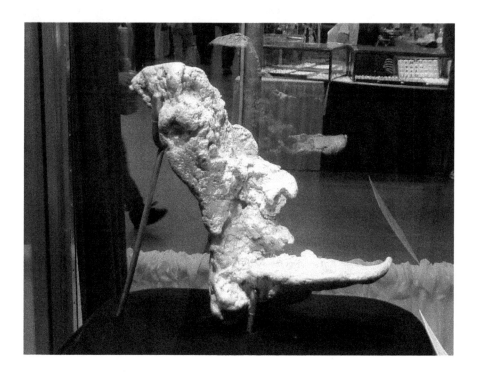

This natural gold nugget was shown in public for this first time at the 2002 Tucson Gem and Mineral Show where it won the prestigious Miguel Romero Memorial Award. Discovered with a metal detector in the Sonora Desert in 1989 it was removed from the earth in pristine condition.

It is the largest placer nugget in existence from the Western Hemisphere and close to 100 oz. larger than the second largest, which was discovered in Alaska.

This unique specimen is considered by many to be the most unusual and beautiful large nugget ever found.

Boot of Cortez
Type: Placer Gold Nugget
Weight: 389.4 Troy Ounces (32.5 Troy Lbs.)
Assay: Approx. 88.6% Pure
Owner: St. Troy Consolidated Mines, Ltd.

Boot of Cortez images courtesy of Robert Boor. The images were taken while the Boot of Cortez was on display at the 2004 Tucson Gem and Mineral Show.

Where Is The Boot of Cortez Now?

On January 20th, 2008, the Boot of Cortez was sold at auction for $1,314,500 or £775,699. As of this writing, this was the most recent transaction for this amazing metal detecting find. Its owner has said that they hope to have it on exhibit soon.

Is There a Metal Detecting Moral to This Story?

I personally believe there is a moral to every story. There is always some sort of knowledge that can be extracted from something like this. In this case, there are two glaring examples that are practically slapping you in the face.

One is the fact that this monster nugget was found with a simple entry level metal detector. The other very important lesson is that slow and steady wins the race. This prospector did not ignore a single target and he took his time making sure every single grain of sand was searched by his metal detector. Incredible and it could happen to you.

Hand of Faith

For this amazing story, we have to travel to the other side of the globe. We have to go "down under" as they say, to the great continent of Australia where food is cooked on the "barbie" and swimming suits are called "budgy smugglers."

This great land just happens to be where the largest gold nugget in the world was found using nothing more than a metal detector by crickey! Okay, I promise not to insert any more Australian slang in the rest of the story mate.

This story takes place in Kingower, Victoria, Australia. This town is no stranger to gold. At one time, the town was quite large during the Victorian Gold Rush. It was the discovery of the Kingower goldfield that brought over 4000 people to the area in a record amount of time.

The area quickly became known for large gold nuggets, and everyone was happily digging them up. That all changed a few years later when the nearby Inglewood goldfield was discovered in 1859.

Everyone pulled up stakes and headed for Inglewood, but a few lucky prospectors stayed behind. They were rewarded with several large nuggets, but the largest of them would not be found until over 120 years later.

Hand of Faith

Kevin Hiller is the lucky man who goes down in the history books for finding the largest gold nugget in the world with a metal detector, and he did it in the Spring of 1980.

Kevin was searching a small area of land behind the old Kingower school house when his metal detector started acting weird. He had been digging all sorts of trash, and he was almost positive that his metal detector was not working properly when he got this signal. It was too erratic and odd. It was as if his machine was falsing.

Frustrated with his detector, Kevin decided to call it a day and ignore that odd signal that made his metal detector act so weird, but he just couldn't get it out of his head. He decided this would be the last thing he dug up that day.

Waiting for him under only six inches of earth was the largest gold nugget ever recovered with a metal detector. Kevin called it, "The Hand of Faith."

Hand of Faith

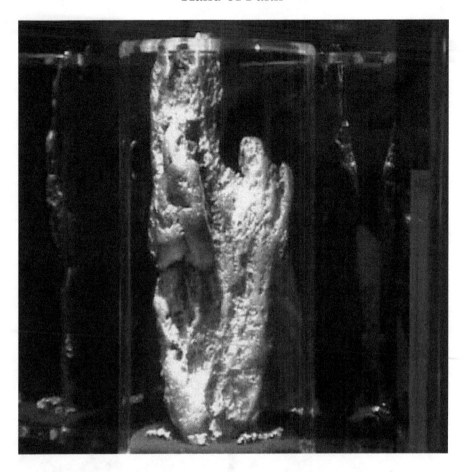

Hand of Faith image courtesy of FF23-fr

his monster sized nugget tips the scales at 45 troy ounces. That is just over 60 pounds or 27.21 kilograms of gold. As they say down under, "What a beauty!"

The unique shape of this huge nugget is how it got its name. It was recovered in a vertical position, and it appeared as if a huge golden hand was reaching up out of the ground to meet Kevin Hiller. Of course, Kevin eagerly reached down to shake this massive golden hand.

What Kind of Metal Detector Was Kevin Using?

Only one metal detector manufacturer can claim their machine was used to uncover one of the largest gold nuggets in the world. Kevin was swinging a Garrett metal detector when he made this discovery. The exact model is not known.

What Happened to the Hand of Faith?

Kevin sold his massive find not long after it was announced during a press conference. The nugget did not stay in its homeland of Australia. It was sold to the Golden Nugget Casino for a cool million dollars where it remains on display in their lobby.

You can feast your eyes on this massive hunk of gold if you happen to be in the Las Vegas area. Here are the details.

Golden Nugget Casino
129 East Fremont St
Las Vegas, NV 89101
Telephone: 702-385-7111

Is There a Metal Detecting Moral to This Story?

If you have spent any amount of time metal detecting, then you may have been told that a particular location has been "hunted out." This phrase implies that all of the treasure has already been found. That wasn't the case in the little town of Kingower.

The largest nugget was found almost 120 years after everyone left the town for what they thought was a more prosperous gold bearing area. Don't ever let anyone tell you an area has been hunted out. There is always a possibility that someone missed the single best piece of treasure in the area.

Destiny

You would think that three massive gold nugget metal detecting finds would be enough, but people are unearthing these massive nuggets all the time. Like the amazing story before this one, this massive nugget was uncovered in Australia where a new type of gold rush has begun. Would be prospectors are busy swinging metal detectors looking for their slice of the golden pie and a prospector by the name of Bill was the lucky one this time.

This story takes place in Ballarat, Australia an area of our planet that is no stranger to large amounts of gold. This area was discovered by a couple of shepherds back in 1837. The shepherds were looking for an area where water was plentiful. A horrible drought was crippling their current pastures. They found what they were looking for in what would later become Ballarat.

For 13 years, shepherds enjoyed the water rich area. Days were spent watching over their flocks and nights were spent counting sheep in their sleep. Things were serene and peaceful. The shepherds found what they considered to be Nirvana! All of that was about to change.

In August of 1851, gold was discovered in the area. This created a gold rush that caused the area to swell like a puppy's belly after a large meal. Thousands of miners descended upon the area like a locust horde of biblical proportions.

In one year alone, over 1000 miners were busy seeking that funny yellow metal. Within three years, the population of miners grew to over 20,000 and they were mining over 20,000 pounds (9000 kilos) of gold in just the first year alone. This is the gold that was legally put onto the books. There was easily just as much gold slipping through the cracks and making its way to the black market.

Care to guess how much gold was discovered here in just the first four years? Over 170,000 pounds or 77,000 kilos. Among this massive load of gold were several very large nuggets.

By 1868, the town was huge. There were over 64,000 miners working for over 300 mining companies. The last mine closed down in 1918 and the busy little mining city slowly diminished down to practically nothing. According to the Ballarat Historical Society, over 20,000,000 troy ounces of gold were mined and recovered from this area.

Like many great treasure stories, a lot of the details of this incredible find are secret. The prospector is simply known as "Bill" and the exact location of the find is only known by a few lucky people.

Bill made his lucky find in some really dense foliage. Trees and large clumps of bushes are always difficult to detect. How are you supposed to get your coil up under all the branches and leaves? Because of this, most people choose to ignore these areas. Bill did not, and he was well rewarded for his efforts because deep under a gnarly mess of thick brush is where he discovered what he would call "Destiny."

Destiny weighs in at 8 pounds or 3.66 kilos. That is one big nugget! You can see the Destiny nugget for yourself at the following web address:

http://www.piecesofvictoria.com/international/wp-content/uploads/2012/09/The-Destiny-Nugget.jpg

What Kind of Metal Detector Was Used?
While a lot of the details surrounding the discovery of Destiny are closely guarded secrets, there is one very important detail that is right out in the open. Bill was using a Minelab GPX-5000 metal detector when he found his monster nugget. Good on ya mate!

What Happened to the Destiny Nugget?
As of this writing, the Destiny nugget is on loan to Sovereign Hill where it is proudly being displayed. Here are the details.

Sovereign Hill
39 Magpie Street
Ballarat, Victoria
3350 Australia

Destiny

Website: http://www.sovereignhill.com.au/

Telephone: 03 5337 1199

What Can We Learn From This Amazing Find?

Once again it seems that persistence pays! Ballarat was a huge mining city that produced tons of gold, but when those veins ran dry, people vanished. There is always treasure to be found no matter how hard an area has been previously hunted. Bill also did something no one else did. He hunted for gold in a place that everyone else ignored. Destiny was found in some dense, thick brush.

The Ausrox Nugget

Australia seems to be leading the way when it comes to big gold nuggets being found with a metal detector. This last gold nugget find proves that point. This story takes place just outside of the townsite known as Ora Banda. The name roughly translates to, "Band of Gold."

Gold was discovered in this area way back in 1893. The area grew and by the year 1910 there were just over 2000 mining families living in the area. Life was not easy for the miners. It was not like they had five star accommodations.

The Ora Banda Hotel which was constructed in 1911 would become the centerpiece for the town. If the walls of this hotel could talk, there would be countless stories worth listening to.

For just over 40 years, the entire area boomed with the discovery of gold, but by the late 1950s things came to a standstill and the centerpiece hotel closed its doors. In 1981, the hotel was restored and reopened. Now it is a popular tourist attraction and a great place to grab a nice cold beer and some authentic local eats.

Today, there are still several gold mining companies working in the area. They are still locating gold, but the mining companies would not be the ones to locate an impressive monster nugget that tipped the scales at over 62

The Ausrox Nugget

troy pounds. That is just over 51 pounds or 23 kilograms. Three local prospectors using metal detectors would be the lucky ones to make this find. Take a look at the Ausrox Nugget.

Photo courtesy the Houston Museum of Natural Science

The Ausrox Nugget

What Happened to This Impressive Nugget?

Much of this incredible find is being kept secret. The three lucky prospectors quickly contacted a local nugget buyer and gave him one week to sell off their incredible find. It only took a couple of days to sell the nugget. The final selling price is also being kept secret.

The nugget was tested and it was confirmed to be 92% pure gold. It's melt value alone would have been worth more than $850,000 or £506,283. Nuggets of this size always sell for two to three times more than their melt value! This nugget is the bloody big one!

Where Is the Ausrox Nugget?

The nugget was sold to an anonymous buyer in the United States. Many people in Australia have expressed outrage over the sale. They want the nugget to remain in Australia. The nugget is currently traveling the world and will be on display in several museums.

These are just a few of the great pieces of gold that have been found using nothing more than a metal detector. There are plenty more that go unreported.

Are there more monster nuggets out there waiting to be found? You can bet there are. Will you be the next person to find one of the monster nuggets using your metal detector? Not if I can beat you to it!

The Treasure Coast

At one point or another every person who has ever held a metal detector in their hands has dreamed about unearthing hoards of treasure. Some of us lie awake at night thinking about it. Some of us drift off to that magical treasure place while we are at work. (Don't worry, I won't tell the boss!)

Some of us manage to find their chest full of silver and gold in their dreams, but along the famed Treasure Coast of Florida there are people who are really finding old pieces of Spanish treasure every single day! This is one treasure story that keeps on giving.

Right now as you read these words there are people metal detecting along a very specific stretch of beach along the east coast of Florida.

One of these people may even be me. I was born and raised in Florida, and I have spent many hours scouring the Treasure Coast in search of old Spanish coins. Have I ever found any lost Spanish coins? Why do you think I keep going back? Finding one old Spanish coin only fuels the desire to uncover more. If there is one, there has to be more and along this stretch of beach there are hundreds of thousands of them. The Treasure Coast of Florida has created dozens of fascinating treasure stories, but why? It all has to do with the 1715 Fleet.

The Treasure Coast

This treasure story starts a very long time ago. In fact, it started over 300 years ago. This was the time in our history when pirates roamed the seas and the Spanish Conquistadors explored, traded and dominated just about every piece of land they came into contact with.

A small fleet of Spanish ships was in route to Mexico. Their cargo consisted of mostly mercury. The mercury was used to refine silver cobs (silver Spanish coins) in Mexico. History books say the name of this fleet was Nueva Espana. This translates to, "New Spain."

This fleet of ships was in Mexico to sell their cargo and pick up Mexican minted silver bars and cobs. The fleet was supposed to depart Mexico, but problem after problem kept the fleet in Mexico for over two years.

The fleet finally managed to leave Mexico where it met with another fleet in Havana. This second fleet was known as Tierra Firme. This second fleet was weighed down with enough treasure to make you wet your pants. Gold and silver from Panama and Cartegena filled the cargo holds of this fleet.

These two fleets combined to make a convoy of 12-13 ships. No one alive seems to know exactly how many ships there were. Several accounts say there were 12 ships, and several others say there were 13 ships. Either way these ships were all loaded with massive amounts of treasure. So much in fact, that the loss of these ships would go down as one of the largest Spanish treasure losses in history.

Records indicate that these ships were carrying only gold and silver. Recent discoveries have proven otherwise. People have been finding exquisite Chinese porcelain, huge gold and silver ingots, beautiful unrefined emeralds, jewel encrusted jewelry, gold coins, silver coins, silverware and more!

More delays would prevent this convoy of heavy ships from leaving Havana in a timely manner. When they did finally depart for Spain it was the month of July. Their route would take them along the east coast of the United States where they followed the Gulf Stream until it turned east and brought them home.

Sailing through the Caribbean and along the east coast of Florida is a great experience during the warmer summer months. The days are long so there is plenty of time under the sun for easy navigating. The waters are cool and inviting and the ocean breeze is soothing enough to lull you right to sleep.

Yes, sailing in the summer is great except for one thing, one very big and very dangerous thing. The summer months belong to hurricane season and these Spanish sailors did not have the convenience of a smartphone in their pocket to warn them about approaching bad weather.

On July 30th, the fleet came head to head with a massive

hurricane. Just imagine for a moment what that must have been like. Being born and raised in Florida makes it very easy for me to imagine just how scary those moments must have been for these Spanish sailors. For those of you who have never had the pleasure of living through a hurricane, let me give you some food for thought.

Your average hurricane will create constant winds well over 130 miles per hour or 241 kilometers per hour. These are not gusts of wind. These are constant destructive winds. These powerful winds can last anywhere from a few hours to a few days. Powerful winds like these are down right frightening to experience on land. They are powerful enough to move vehicles, snap giant trees like toothpicks, blow the roof clean off a house and create all types of deadly high speed projectiles. You don't want to be outside in this type of wind let alone on the deck of a ship in the Atlantic ocean.

The wind is not the only problem either. Hurricanes create torrential amounts of rain. The rain mixed with the powerful wind can not only make it difficult to see, but it can be very painful!

Let's not forget the occasional lightning strike. Lightning is attracted to tall objects like trees and ship masts! This all sounds pretty bad doesn't it? Well it gets worse, much worse.

Hurricanes can also spawn tornadoes. Notice that word is

plural? Not only do you have to deal with the dangerous winds, torrential downpours and deadly lightning, but you also have to deal with the possibility of multiple tornadoes all at the same time! Living through this type of experience on land is difficult. Surviving it on a ship is next to impossible.

Boats have one more thing to deal with. They have to deal with the fury of the sea. I have seen the ocean during a hurricane with my own two eyes. It is bone chilling. It will make you realize just how small you are in the grand scheme of our wonderful planet. What was once a blue oasis of inviting water is now a massive mess of water and waves that have no logical pattern.

The ocean comes to life and the waves can surge as high as 50 feet. One wall of water after another smashes into itself, the land, the trees and anything else that is unfortunate enough to get in its way. You can't stop moving water. Waves of this magnitude will destroy anything in their path.

The Treasure Coast

Now that you have the details. Try to imagine what it must have been like for these Spanish sailors in their ships that were already overloaded with massive amounts of treasure. Devastating winds, torrential rains, lightning, tornadoes and the fury of the sea sank every single ship in this convoy. Every piece of treasure these ships were carrying was now scattered along the east coast of Florida. The treasure loss is one thing, but thousands of innocent lives were lost as well.

The lone survivors made camps along the beach where they started salvaging as much treasure as they could. The Spanish would later take part in a recovery mission that would last 2-3 years. They built a large camp along the shores of the ocean, and with the help of local Indians they were able to recover a large amount of the treasure.

The Big Discovery
The treasure has managed to make its way all over the
state of Florida. Pieces of it have been found far inland
where local Indian tribes carried it along their daily routes,
but the real history started to get uncovered in the 1950s
when Kip Wagner found a piece of eight on the beach after
a hurricane.

Kip put two and two together, consulted some older charts
and maps and picked up an early model army surplus
metal detector that was primarily used for locating land
mines. Kip was able to locate the original Spanish
recovery camp where he unearthed gold and silver coins,
relics and pottery. The next logical step was to try and get
a bird's eye view of the area.

Kip rented an airplane to help spot the wreckage of the
ships. From his airplane view, he could see what looked
like ships under the ocean. Kip, along with the state of
Florida began salvaging the area by boat. They dove the
waters and located hundreds of thousands of coins and
other treasures. All of the coins they managed to pull from
the ocean were in excellent condition.

This entire area has become a huge source of treasure for
many eager treasure hunters. There are countless great
stories from the past, and there are more being made every
single time the weather in the area takes a turn for the

worst.

Get Your Share of the Treasure

There is nothing stopping you from claiming your share of treasure in this amazing story, but there are a few things to consider before you embark on your treasure hunt. A waterproof metal detector that has been designed to work on the beach is going to be your best bet at finding any coins, but you can't legally use a machine in the waters here. You can only detect on the beach from the edge of the dunes down to the low tide line. You can't use a metal detector in the water, and you can't use one in the dunes either.

You should also plan your visit around any type of weather event. It could be a winter Nor'easter, or it could be a summer tropical storm or a hurricane. These types of weather events move a lot of sand and help to expose the older heavy gold and silver coins beneath. People do find coins and other pieces of treasure during any time of the year, and there have been people who have found treasure using nothing more than their eyes.

If you do go after a storm event, you can bet that you won't be alone. Eager treasure hunters descend upon this beach in droves. There are so many of them that you may find it difficult to swing your coil!

Where Should You Go?

The Treasure Coast starts just below Sebastian Inlet and extends almost all the way down to West Palm Beach. Just remember to fill in your holes, stay out of state parks, the dunes and the water. This is one treasure story where you get to be the star. Have fun and get some treasure of your own!

The Treasure Coast

I could give you a more detailed map with very specific GPS coordinates, but an old pirate friend of mine would most likely keel haul me, and I don't feel like spending my final moments strapped to the hull of a pirate ship.

350 Year Old Golden Chalice

Florida's fabulous treasure coast is not the only coastline rich with treasure history. Just about any shoreline can have buried treasure. There are countless shipwrecks and past civilizations on pretty much every coastline in the world.

This awesome story takes place in the southern straits of Florida on a little chain of coral ridden islands known as the Florida Keys where the clear blue waters were a favorite among pirates and early Spanish explorers whose ships were almost always overloaded with treasure.

Enter the Treasure Hunter
20 year old Mike DeMar a former resident of Seattle, Washington moves to Key West, Florida to pursue a lifelong dream of finding buried treasure. He joined up with a salvage company by the name of Blue Water Ventures Key West, a joint venture partner of Mel Fisher's Treasures.

Blue Water Ventures Key West had been actively searching an area of the keys for over three years. They were searching for a galleon so overloaded with treasure that it weighed 480 tons. Like many other shipwrecks of this era, the galleon was carrying a little too much treasure.

A ship plump with treasure and a fierce storm always wind

up becoming a deadly scenario and that is exactly what sealed the fate of this galleon. On board the ship were 143 passengers and an unfathomable amount of treasure.

Just four months into his treasure seeking adventures, Mike would make the find of a lifetime. It makes sense that this guy would find treasure in the ocean. His last name means "of the sea."

Equipped with scuba tanks and waterproof metal detectors, team members scour the bottom of the shallow waters. They have made plenty of discoveries in the past and they know this area is rich in more than undersea life. Mike was in 18 feet of water when his metal detector signaled something buried beneath the sand.

Mike's first thought was an old beer can. It would not be the first one they had found. Unfortunately beer cans litter the floor of the ocean and they are something you have to deal with when you are hunting treasure.

Using his hands, Mike started to fan the bottom. With each wave of his hand, a small layer of sand was pushed aside until he had revealed a hole about 1 foot or .3 meters deep, and there it was staring him right in the face. An ornate golden chalice that was over 350 years old.

Initial reports say the chalice is easily worth a million dollars. That is £595,593 for you British folks. This incredible find is proof that lifelong dreams can come true

350 Year Old Golden Chalice

as long as you put forth the effort to pursue them!

You can see this magnificent golden chalice for yourself at the following web address:

http://www.melfisher.com/goldchalice.asp

The Ringlemere Cup

The golden chalice found off the coast of the Florida Keys is certainly not the only golden cup in existence, and it is definitely not the only golden cup to be unearthed. This great find takes place across the pond in the historic town of Sandwich, England. Just curious here, but what do you think they eat for lunch in Sandwich?

In 2001, Cliff Bradshaw was searching a recently plowed field with his metal detector. It just so happens that Cliff is an "amateur" archeologist who has a fond interest in the Anglo-Saxon period.

For a period of over a year he carefully searched through a field where he was regularly finding artifacts. He knew his finds were not just random. He knew that this field must have had some sort of historical significance for the Anglo-Saxon period. If he was correct, then there had to be an ancient Anglo-saxon burial mound nearby.

Cliff noticed a slight raised area in the field. This had to be the burial mound. He immediately started searching the outside perimeter of the mound. He knew he would have a better chance of recovering treasure in the shallower sides of the burial mound.

It did not take him long to locate his first target, an Anglo-Saxon gilded brooch. It was buried a mere 8-10 inches or

20-25 centimeters below the surface. Of course this find excited him immensely. He continued to slowly search the outer perimeter of the burial mound. This is where he made the important discovery of what would be called the Ringlemere Cup.

Image courtesy of portableantiquities (Dominic Coyne, Young Graduates for Museums and Galleries Programme, British Museum)

The Ringlemere Cup

The cup was badly damaged by a recent plow, but Cliff knew he was standing on top of something that would change history. He immediately called the local authorities who would later precisely excavate the entire burial mound.

A Controversy Develops

Cliff believed this site was Anglo-Saxon, but archeologists kept saying otherwise. Every other archeologist on the site said there was just no possible way this could be an Anglo-Saxon burial site. They all insisted it was a Bronze Age Barrow, but Cliff refused to believe them. He knew better. This controversy went on for a period of three years. Of course the professional archeologists knew better than some "amateur" swinging a metal detector.

This would all change in 2004 when other Anglo-Saxon burials were found on the same site just south of where Cliff made his original find. It seems he was right all along.

I almost forgot to mention. That golden cup he found was declared treasure. The value of this treasure was £270,000 or $520,000. Not bad for an "amateur" archeologist with a metal detector, huh?

As of this writing, the Ringlemere cup was on display at The British Museum.

Hoards

Hoard: A stock or store of money or valued objects, typically one that is secret or carefully guarded.

By definition alone, a hoard is something that every person with a metal detector is looking for. Wouldn't you agree? It can be great finding one or two older coins, but finding a hoard is something that most of us dream of!

It just so happens that people lucky enough to live in Europe are the ones finding these long lost treasures, and you will be amazed when you learn just how many hoards have been located and unearthed using nothing more than a metal detector.

My first guess would be in the neighborhood of maybe a dozen or so. As of this writing, there have been over 50 documented hoard discoveries over the years. If this many have been found and documented, just imagine how many hoards must still exist out there. You could be the next person to find one! What follows are some of the best metal detecting hoard finds.

The Hoxne Hoard

This incredible find has a really great story behind it. A local farm hand by the name of Peter Whatling lost a hammer while working. He decided to get in touch with a friend who owned a metal detector to help him find his lost hammer.

His friend, a retired gardener by the name of Eric Lawes was the obvious choice. What they found would wind up changing history.

During their initial search of the field, they discovered silver spoons, several pieces of gold jewelry, gold coins and silver coins as well. The two knew they had made a huge discovery so they called in the local authorities.

A team of archeologists was dispatched to the area and the entire hoard was removed in one day. The archeologists also used metal detectors to help them uncover the final pieces of the hoard.

Why this huge hoard of treasure was buried will never be known.

What Was Found?
This is a big one! 14,865 gold, silver and bronze Roman coins. The hoard also included over 200 additional pieces of treasure which included tableware and gold jewelry. In

The Hoxne Hoard

total, the Hoxne Hoard equaled 3.5 kilograms (That is 7.7 pounds for the Americans) of gold and 23.75 kilograms (That is 52.4 pounds) of silver. Could you imagine finding this with your metal detector? Here is a breakdown of this incredible find.

- 569 gold coins
- 14,272 silver coins
- 24 bronze coins
- 29 pieces of gold jewelry
- 98 pieces of silver tableware (spoons and ladles)
- An intricate silver tigress
- 4 silver bowls and one small silver dish
- one silver beaker
- a silver vase
- 4 pepper pots
- 2 silver locks
- a small ivory pyxis (a small round box used to hold women's cosmetics)

Check out the pictures of this incredible find!

The Hoxne Hoard

This image is a reconstructed version of the box the hoard
was originally found in.
Image courtesy of Mike Peel (www.mikepeel.net).

Four golden bracelets that were part of the hoard.
Image courtesy of Mike Peel (www.mikepeel.net).

The Hoxne Hoard

The intricate silver tigress
Image courtesy of http://www.flickr.com/photos/lindas_pictures/

A fabulous gold body chain that was also part of the hoard.
Image courtesy of Mike Peel (www.mikepeel.net).

Whew! I need to catch my breath after looking at those pictures.

The Hoxne Hoard

What Was It Worth?
£3.02 million or $4,983,000

When Was the Hoard Discovered?
November 16th 1992

Where Was the Hoard Discovered?
Southwest of the village of Hoxne in Suffolk, England

Where Is It Now?
The British Museum acquired the Hoxne Hoard in April of 1994.

Interesting Facts About The Hoxne Hoard
The entire hoard was found in what was left of a large wooden box that could be thought of as a treasure chest. This discovery helped changed the local laws about metal detecting and finds that have a significant archeological significance. As of this writing, this is the single largest hoard of Roman silver and gold coins found in Britain.

The Frome Hoard

What Was Found?
A clay pot with 52,503 1800 year old Roman coins made from silver and bronze. The coins date back to AD 253 to 293.

Image courtesy of Portable Antiquities Scheme from London, England

What Was It Worth?
£320,000 or $531,520

When Was the Hoard Discovered?
April 2010

The Frome Hoard

Where Was the Hoard Discovered?
In a field in the southwestern region of England known as
Frome, Somerset.

Who Found It?
63 year old Dave Crisp was the one lucky enough to find
this amazing hoard. Find out more about this hoard and
Dave's other great finds in his book. You can find it in the
UK Amazon store.

http://www.amazon.co.uk/Metal-Detecting-need-know-
started/dp/1897738471

Where Is It Now?
The hoard was on display in 2011 at the Museum of
Somerset.

Interesting Facts About The Frome Hoard
As difficult as it seems, once Dave knew that his find was
much more than 21 roman coins, he chose to leave the
entire hoard in the ground until some archeologists could
arrive and properly excavate it. That is one decision that no
one could take lightly.

The Frome hoard would wind up being the largest find of
coins in a single pot in the UK.

The Vale of York Hoard

What Was Found?

A total of 617 silver coins that were later discovered to be from a 10th century Viking Hoard. The coins were not the only items found. There were also ingots, ornaments, precious metals, hacksilver and a gold arm band.

Image courtesy of Portable Antiquities Scheme from London, England

The Vale of York Hoard

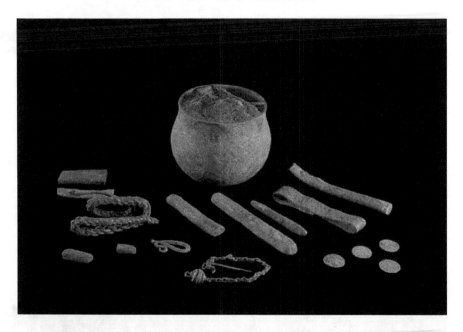

Image courtesy of Portable Antiquities Scheme from London, England

Image courtesy of Jmiall

The Vale of York Hoard

The entire hoard was found in a bowl lined with fine silver and gold leaf. The outside of the bowl has a brilliant decorative pattern with vines, leaves and six different hunting scenes depicting lionesses.

Image courtesy of vintagedept from Olen (London), Belgium (United Kingdom)

A true historical work of art. Could you imagine finding something like this with your metal detector?

What Was It Worth?
Are you sitting down for this one? The Vale of York Hoard has been valued at £1,082,000 or $1,797,202

When Was the Hoard Discovered?

The Vale of York Hoard

January 6th 2007

Where Was the Hoard Discovered?
It was found in an unploughed field near Harrogate, England.

Who Found It?
David Whelan and his son Andrew. What a father and son moment that must have made! They had both been metal detecting for about five years before making this incredible find.

Where Is It Now?
The hoard is sitting pretty in the British Museum or Yorkshire museum.

Interesting Facts About The Vale of York Hoard
The entire hoard was buried in some type of lead container. This outer shell helped protect the hoard. As of this writing, this is the largest Viking hoard found in Britain since 1840.

Staffordshire Hoard

The Staffordshire Hoard consists of right around 3,500 Anglo-Saxon gold and silver pieces that include weapon decorations, jewelry and crosses. The total weights are 5 kilograms (11 pounds) of gold and 1.3 kilograms (2.9 pounds) of silver.

The weapon decorations include: gold and silver sword hilt collars and sword pommels with garnets and intricate inlays.

Three crosses were found in the hoard as well. One of the crosses was folded and another was missing most of the decorative settings.

The hoard also contained an amazing gold strip inscribed in Latin. The inscription reads "SURGE DNE DISEPENTUR INIMICI TUI ET FUGENT QUI ODERUNT TE A FACIE TUA."

The translation reads, "Rise up Lord may your enemies be scattered and those who hate you be driven from your face." What an absolutely incredible historical find, and just think, without a metal detector these items may have never been discovered.

Here are a few items from the hoard.

Staffordshire Hoard

Image courtesy of David Rowan, Birmingham Museum and Art Gallery

hat Was It Worth?
£3.285 million or $5,315,200

When Was the Hoard Discovered?
July 5th 2009

Where Was the Hoard Discovered?
In a recently plowed field near Lichfield, Staffordshire,
England

Who Found It?
Over a period of five days, one lucky individual by the

name of Terry Herbert found enough gold items to fill 244 bags. At this point he contacted the authorities and Fred Johnson, the current land owner allowed the field to be excavated.

Image courtesy of Portable Antiquities Scheme from London, England

Terry Herbert looking over some of the hoard.

Two more excavations were carried out in 2010 and 2012 producing even more historical finds.

Where Is It Now?
Pieces of the hoard are now scattered across various

museums all over Britain. At the time of this writing, the following museums had individual pieces of this hoard on display:

- Birmingham Museum & Art Gallery
- The British Museum
- Potteries Museum & Art Gallery
- Stoke-On-Trent

Interesting Facts About The Staffordshire Hoard
This hoard was so significant, that historians have had to re-examine their earlier theories of Anglo-Saxon England. The entire hoard and location were initially kept secret in order to prevent thieves from disturbing the fragile archaeological finds.

The Hallaton Hoard

This hoard was originally known as the Southeast Leicestershire Treasure, but it is now being called the Hallaton Treasure. It consists of over 5,294 silver and gold Roman coins, jewelry, a decorative mount, a silver bowl, two ingots, over 7,000 animal bone pieces, a Roman Parade helmet originally covered in silver sheeting and gold leaf. Inside the helmet were 7 cheekpieces. Check this stuff out!

The Hallaton Hoard

Image courtesy of Portable Antiquities Scheme from London, England
Coins from the hoard

The Hallaton Hoard

The Roman Parade helmet was removed in what is known as "block format." The archeologists removed a large square chunk of earth with the helmet still inside. This gave them the opportunity to properly conserve the piece. It took the British Museum 9 years to properly remove and conserve the entire helmet.

Image courtesy of Portable Antiquities Scheme from London, England
The parade helmet

Image courtesy of Prioryman
One of the cheekpieces found with the hoard

Archeologists believe that the area was a shrine of some sort where animals were being offered. 97% of all the animal bones found were from pigs, and most of them were buried whole.

The Hallaton Hoard

What Was It Worth?
The value of this hoard is still being determined. The helmet alone has been valued at £650,000 or $1,081,795.

When Was the Hoard Discovered?
November 19th 2000

Where Was the Hoard Discovered?
Close to Hallaton in southeast Leicestershire, England

Who Found It?
Ken Wallace found the first 130 coins with his metal detector. He reported the find to the authorities and the rest of the hoard was found by the Hallaton Fieldwork Group.

Where Is It Now?
At the time of this writing, portions of this hoard were on display at the Harborough Museum.

The Salisbury Hoard

This particular hoard has a very interesting story. Apparently this is one hoard that was uncovered by two metal detectorists secretly and illegally. The discovery began in the year 1988 when an archaeologist by the name of Dr. Ian Stead came across a few pieces of the hoard. He was fascinated by these pieces, but he had no idea where they had come from.

He started doing some investigating because he saw the importance of the pieces. He knew they were Iron Age bronze artifacts. His investigations led him to several rumors that there were hundreds of pieces floating around the black market. It took Dr. Ian several years and several secret pub meetings to uncover the full story.

All of his hard investigative work paid off. All of the items that have been recovered date back over 2000 years. It is believed that some of the items were already 2000 years old when they were first buried. That means that some of the artifacts are over 4000 years old!

Most of the items were found in a huge pit. It is believed that these miniature items were offerings to ancient gods.

It is unfortunate that these items were all recovered illegally. Had they been properly recovered, there may have been even more interesting information regarding the find.

What Was Found?
Over 600 prehistoric bronze metal objects. All of the pieces in this hoard are miniature versions of full sized weapons and shields.

Where Is It Now?
The British Museum

St. Albans Hoard

Wesley Carrington's story is the perfect example of beginner's luck. Wesley knew he wanted to try hunting for treasure, but he did not want to spend a lot of money on a metal detector. He purchased the cheapest entry level machine he could find. His purchase would prove to be a worthwhile investment because just 20 minutes into his very first hunt, Wesley made the find of a lifetime: a hoard of gold roman coins.

When he found the initial batch of 40 coins, he brought them back to the shop where he originally purchased his metal detector. He was not sure what he should do with them. The shop owner knew that this was indeed a rare and incredible find, and he contacted the local authorities. Another search of the area unearthed another 119 coins.

What Was Found?
159 gold solidi Roman coins that are more than 1600 years old!

What Was It Worth?
The value of this hoard is still being determined, but single gold solidis have sold for as much as £1000 or $1663.80 at auction. That could put the total value at £159,000 or $264,544

When Was the Hoard Discovered?

St. Albans Hoard

2012

Where Was the Hoard Discovered?
The hoard was found near St Albans Hertfordshire.

Where Is It Now?
St. Albans' Verulamium Museum

The Stirling Hoard

David Booth's story is yet another excellent example of beginner's luck. His amazing find also proves that you don't always need an expensive metal detector to locate buried treasure. The model he used to make this incredible find was an entry level machine with a relatively small price tag.

David set out treasure hunting the right way. He spent some time investigating an area he thought may have potential for treasure. The area he was interested in was a field located in Scotland.

The next step for David was to contact the owner of the land and obtain permission to hunt and that is exactly what David did.

When he arrived at the location, he parked right outside of the field. The area looked perfect for treasure hunting and David was eager to try out his new metal detector.

Being his first time using his new machine, David thought it would be a good idea to try it out on an area of flat ground right behind his car. He took about 7 steps, turned on his metal detector and this is what he found.

Image courtesy of Johnbod
One of four Torcs found

Could you imagine finding something like this the very first time you took your metal detector out for a hunt or any time for that matter? This is the stuff dreams are made of.

What Was Found?
Four gold Iron Age torcs.

What Was It Worth?
£462,000 or $768,167. I think David more than paid for his entry level metal detector with this find. He might as well

retire from the hobby of metal detecting and let me or you grab the next great piece of treasure.

When Was the Hoard Discovered?
September 20th 2009

Where Was the Hoard Discovered?
Blair Drummond, Stirlingshire, Scotland

Where Is It Now?
National Museums Scotland

Wickham Market Hoard

Not every amazing treasure find happens when a first timer fires up their metal detector. Some people metal detect for years before they make that huge life altering find. This is the case with Michael Dark and the Wickham Market Hoard.

Michael is no newcomer to the world of metal detecting. In fact, it took him 25 years of searching to locate his first gold coin. He knew there had to be more gold coins buried in the ground nearby.

Determined to find more of the coins, Michael returned to the spot where he recovered the first. The hunting conditions were horrible, but gold fever had already taken hold of Michael.

It was cold, windy and sleet was pelting him. Like any metal detecting enthusiast who is on the hunt, Michael ignored the weather conditions and continued his search. As luck would have it, his search produced eight more gold coins. These eight additional gold coins were not enough. The gold had made its way into Michael's heart. One look in his eyes and it was easy to see Michael had developed a mild case of gold fever.

Michael's metal detector suddenly went nuts. From the sound of it, there was something really big buried right beneath his feet. Could it be even more of the gold coins? His mild case of gold fever was now escalated to the point of no return. He knew he was standing on a huge pile of gold coins. Here is where the story takes an odd turn.

Instead of recovering his find, Michael decided he would have to leave it over night. That's right. Michael decided that it was in his best interest to return and uncover his find after a good night's rest. He used rocks to mark the location on the ground and went home, cleaned up and went to sleep. Wait a minute? WHAT?????

I don't know about you, but there is simply no way I could have done this, but to each their own I suppose.

When he returned, he uncovered another 774 gold coins bringing the total amount of gold coins to 840! And just think, Michael let those additional 774 gold coins lay in the ground one more night. What harm could come from letting them stay buried for one more night?

Wickham Market Hoard

Image courtesy of Portable Antiquities Scheme from London, England

What Was It Worth?
£316,000 or $525,413

When Was the Hoard Discovered?
March 2008

Where Was the Hoard Discovered?
Dallinghoo near Wickham Market, Suffolk, England

Where Is It Now?
Ipswich Museum

The Bredon Hill Hoard

Jethro Carpenter and Mark Gilmour are no strangers to metal detecting and this is no case of beginner's luck either. The two treasure hunters were hunting an area of private farm land where they made some interesting finds in the past. The farm land would prove fruitful yet again when their machine gave them a good strong signal.

Excited to locate their newly found piece of treasure, the two treasure hunters started to unearth their find. Wouldn't you know it. There was no real treasure waiting for them in that hole they just excavated. The piece of treasure was nothing more than a old rusty nail.

In my book entitled: "Metal Detecting: A Beginner's Guide to Mastering the Greatest Hobby In the World," I talk about the importance of always scanning your holes twice. This story drives this fact straight home.

After removing the nail, Jethro and Mark scanned the hole again. There were still more targets in the hole. As they kept digging, they started noticing pottery shards. It wasn't long until they started finding coins, lots of coins. They knew they had just found a huge hoard and thought it would be best to report it to the authorities.

The coins in this particular hoard are very interesting because each coin is made from a very small amount of silver. It is estimated that most of the coins are only about 1% silver. This was done intentionally to devalue the coins when they were created.

What Was Found?
3784 silver Roman coins

Image courtesy of portableantiquities

The Bredon Hill Hoard

Image courtesy of portableantiquities
Jethro Carpenter and Mark Gilmour along with Richard Henry from the Portable Antiquities Scheme.

What Was It Worth?
At the time of this writing, the value of this hoard was still being investigated.

When Was the Hoard Discovered?
June 18th 2011

Where Was the Hoard Discovered?
On a farm in Bredon Hill Worcestershire, England

Where Is It Now?
At the time of this writing, the Worcester City Art Gallery & Museum was trying to purchase the hoard.

The Chalgrove Hoards

That is not a typo. The word hoards in this particular find is supposed to be plural, and would you believe that both of these hoards were found by the same person 14 years apart?

Some people believe that locating a huge hoard of coins is a once in a lifetime achievement. Brian Miller has proved them otherwise by locating both of these incredible hoards with a metal detector. While both hoards are quite spectacular, the second hoard held an ancient clue that would have historians scratching their heads in wonder.

Brian brought all of the coins to the Ashmolean Museum fused in a giant ball still in the original container. Brian knew he had another fantastic find on his hands, but he had no idea what was hiding inside that old ball of Roman coins.

The British Museum was in charge of cleaning the coins, and in February of 2004 they found one coin inside the hoard that would change history. On the face of this mysterious coin was an unknown emperor.

A coin just like this one was found in France 100 years earlier, but experts claimed the coin was a hoax because there was no record of this mysterious emperor. This one coin proved that this emperor did indeed exist. His name was Domitianus, and he only ruled the land for a few days.

The Chalgrove Hoards

His short reign over the Roman empire proved that control changed hands pretty quickly. This coin has been called the single most significant coin find in all of Britain history. Just think about that for a second. This single most important historical coin find in Britain was found using a metal detector!

What Was Found?
Hoard # 1 consisted of 4145 Roman coins.
Hoard # 2 consisted of 4957 Roman coins.

Image courtesy of Portable Antiquities Scheme from London, England

The Chalgrove Hoards

When Was the Hoard Discovered?
Hoard # 1 was discovered in August 1989.
Hoard # 2 was discovered 14 years later in 2003.

Where Was the Hoard Discovered?
Both hoards were discovered in close proximity to each other. They were only 100 feet or 30 meters apart. They were both found on farmland in Chalgrove, England.

Who Found It?
The first hoard was found by a father and son metal detecting team, Brian and Ian Miller. The second hoard was found by Brian Miller.

The Shrewsbury Hoard

Yet another instance where a huge hoard was found by someone who just started metal detecting. Nic Davies had only been metal detecting for about a month, and this hoard was his first find. Could this have been beginner's luck?

Nic did make one huge mistake though. He found the hoard while trespassing on private land. He did not have permission to metal detect and as a result, there is a really good chance he will not receive any monetary reward for this great find.

The current treasure laws in Britain state that should a hoard be classified as treasure, a reward will be paid to the landowner and the person responsible for finding the hoard as long as the person searching was not doing so without permission.

Always get permission before you hunt private property, and make sure you have permission in writing!

What Was Found?
9315 bronze Roman coins.

The Shrewsbury Hoard

Image courtesy of Portable Antiquities Scheme from London, England

The Shrewsbury Hoard

When Was the Hoard Discovered?
August 2009

Where Was the Hoard Discovered?
Shrewsbury, Shropshire, England

Who Found It?
Nic Davies.

Where Is It Now?
The British Museum is in charge of cleaning the coins, but the Shropshire County Museum is trying to acquire the hoard.

The Derrynaflan Hoard

The father and son team who found this hoard supposedly obtained permission to hunt the ancient monastic site of Derrynaflan, but they did not have permission to dig on the land. The area was protected under the National Monuments Act of 1930. This act protected the land and prohibited any type of digging.

When the father and son team made their incredible find, they kept it hidden for three weeks. The find was deemed illegal and the father and son team fought in court for over 7 years. They claimed their find was worth £5,000,000 or $8,377,500. Because they did not have any proof that they had permission to dig, they were never able to legally claim the find. OUCH! As a result of the claim lasting 7 years, the Irish laws of treasure trove were changed.

Once again, always get permission in writing before your dig on private property, and never attempt to dig on any type of national monument!

What Was Found?
- A beautiful chalice
- A silver paten. A paten is a small plate made from silver or gold.
- A hoop
- A liturgical strainer
- A bronze basin

The Derrynaflan Hoard

Here are a few items from this awesome find.

Image courtesy of Kglavin
The chalice from the hoard

The Derrynaflan Hoard

Image courtesy of Kglavin
The paten or silver and gold plate from the hoard

When Was the Hoard Discovered?
February 17th 1980

Where Was the Hoard Discovered?
This hoard was found on an island of pastureland off the coast of Ireland near Killenaule, South Tipperary.

Who Found It?
Michael Webb and his son.

Where Is It Now?
The National Museum of Ireland

The Grouville Hoard

Not all great treasures are found by first timer rookies, and this hoard is the perfect example. Reg Mead and Richard Miles were two lucky ones in this story. The two treasure hunters researched an area they thought would be perfect for metal detecting. Upon asking permission to hunt, the land owner told them a very interesting story.

A few years earlier while plowing the field, the land owner came across an earthenware pot filled with silver coins. His plow brought them to the surface and scattered them across the field. When Reg and Richard heard this story, their eyes grew wide with excitement.

The land owner granted two treasure hunters permission to hunt, but under very strict circumstances. The land owner would only let the two guys use their metal detectors once a year for about 10-15 hours after the crops had been harvested.

Obviously this didn't give the two eager treasure hunters much time to locate any amount of treasure, but they did not let that stop them. It would take them over 30 years to locate this unbelievable find.

On that fateful day in the summer of 2012, Reg and Richard eagerly followed a trail of 60 silver coins. That trail would eventually lead them to one gold coin, but

those 61 coins were just the icing on the cake. They were
the tip of the iceberg! They were nothing compared to
what came next!

The next target was big. It was huge. It was massive! All of
these phrases are understatements. The next target was a
mass of coins that weighed an eye popping 1650 pounds or
750 kilograms. They quickly alerted the authorities who
sent out a team of archeologists to remove the coins.

Here is what they found!
An estimated 70,000 silver and gold Roman coins and
some jewelry.

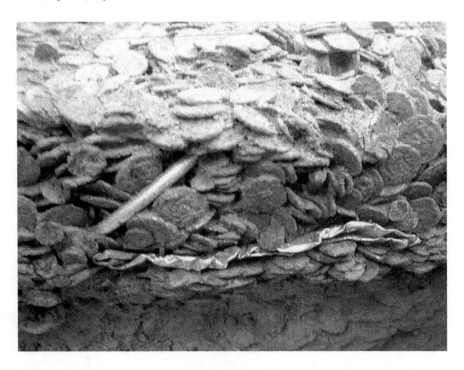

If you look closely, you can see two gold torcs in the giant coin mass.

What Was It Worth?

At the time of this writing, the value was still being determined. Each coin could fetch as much as £100 - £200 or $167 - $335. That means the entire hoard would be worth more than £7,000,000 or $11,756,500.00. Holy great finds!

Where Was the Hoard Discovered?

The parish of Grouville on the east side of Jersey in the Channel Islands. No, this is not New Jersey in America.

Where Is It Now?

The hoard is currently being valued and cleaned. It is expected to be on display at the Jersey Museum sometime in the year 2014.

Never give up! Just imagine if these two had decided to call it quits.

All of these hoards are incredible finds, and the ones I have included account for a very small number of hoards that have currently been found using nothing more than a metal detector. There are plenty more out there waiting for you to dig them up.

Frightening Finds

Frightening Finds

With metal detector in hand we busily comb through parks, lakes, rivers, oceans, fields, woods or forests scanning for bits of history that we call treasure. Those lost pieces of treasure could be anywhere, and every single piece of treasure no matter how big or small comes with some sort of history attached to it. It is only a matter of time until some poor unfortunate soul manages to dig up some treasure that comes with a darker history. A history that should have stayed buried.

I have recovered a few somewhat "creepy" finds myself. A tooth here. An entire set of teeth there and even human bones. Granted these finds were nothing like the stories that follow. Although I will admit that each one of them sent a chill down my spine. There is nothing quite like seeing an entire set of teeth laying in the bottom of your beach scoop as you stand neck deep in dark murky water. Once you realize what it is, your mind starts to wander. It leaves you with an unsettling feeling to say the least.

Let's take a trip to the darker side of metal detecting and uncover some real life finds that have made full grown men think twice about digging again. Some of these stories are a little on the dark side. Consider this your warning. If this sort of thing bothers you, then you may want to skip over these true frightening metal detecting stories.

Page 96

The Beach of Death

Let's start this section off with a personal story of my own that left me feeling a little uncomfortable.

One of my favorite places to metal detect is the beach. When conditions are right, there is nothing to complain about. You have the beauty of the ocean, the warm sun, bikini clad beauties and miles of treasure producing sand. That is not what the beach conditions were like on this day.

I was hunting a small stretch of beach on the east coast of Florida. Even in the winter, you could usually wear a pair of shorts and a t-shirt while hunting, but this day would be a little different.

There was a cold front that was supposed to move through the area in a few days. As usual, the weatherman was a wee bit inaccurate. (no offense to any meteorologists who may be reading this) The cold front made a overnight surprise visit, and of course this caused the temperatures to drop quite significantly. I would not be able to hunt in a pair of shorts and a t-shirt. I would need shoes, long pants and a jacket if I wanted to hunt comfortably in this cold weather.

I arrived at the beach two hours before low tide. This should give me plenty of time to comb through the wet sand. When I walked onto the beach, I could not believe my eyes. There were dead fish everywhere. They were so thick on the beach that it became difficult to walk. It was even more difficult to swing a metal detector.

Apparently the cold front caught all of the local fish by surprise as well. Normally these fish would have migrated south to much warmer waters, but this freak cold front caught them all off guard and killed them.

These were no baby fish either. There were some that were as long as my leg and as big around as my torso. Some of these dead fish would have been record breakers had they been caught on a fishing pole.

Still to this day, I have never seen anything quite like this. For miles down the beach, there were thousands of dead fish. Did that stop me from metal detecting? Of course not!

I meandered through the beach of death swinging my metal detector in between all of the fish carcasses. I noticed a few low spots on the beach and made my way towards them.

I started getting signals as soon as I got to the first low spot. I was happily digging up modern coins among all the dead fish. If there was a dead fish in the way, I would just move it with my scoop.

The next signal my metal detector gave me put a huge smile on my face. It was a solid low tone. On the particular machine I was using at the time, this solid low tone was usually a piece of gold.

I moved a few fish carcasses aside and put the point of my scoop into the beach sand. I stood on the back of my scoop and watched it sink. I removed a giant scoop of sand and scanned the hole with my metal detector. The target was still in the hole.

A foul odor filled the air. It was difficult to describe, but it made me feel uneasy. The foul odor was coming from the hole I had just made. This didn't make me feel any better. I contemplated covering the hole and moving on, but the thought of a gold ring (my precious) kept me digging.

I pushed my scoop down into the hole and retrieved yet another pile of beach sand. I scanned the hole again. There was no signal from the hole. I had my target in my scoop.

I dumped the sand and lightly kicked it across the beach. I ran my detector over the sand and pinpointed the signal. It was still buried under a few inches of sand. I lightly spread the sand across the beach with my foot. In the middle of the sand was a small black disc about the size of an American quarter.

This was no gold. It did not look familiar at all. I reached down and picked it up. It was still covered in sand. With a quick puff, I blew the sand away. It was at that precise moment that I realized exactly what I held in my hand. It

The Beach of Death

was a crematory tag. A chill went down my spine. These are the tags that are used to identify human ashes when a person is cremated. It had been tossed into the ocean along with a person's ashes.

Here I was standing on the beach surrounded by thousands of dead fish holding a crematory tag in my hand. I reached back and threw the crematory tag as far as I could into the ocean. It skipped across the ocean like a rock until it finally sank back to the bottom. At this point, I decided to call it quits and head back home.

On the way back to my car, I came across this weird dead fish. It is a Mora Mora or a sunfish. What a perfect ending for such an odd day of detecting on the beach.

The Beach of Death

The Dark Treasure of Little Bighorn

On June 25th and 26th close to the Little Bighorn River in Montana, a brutal battle took place. This battle would be known as "Custer's Last Stand," and it went down in the history books as the single most devastating conflict of the Great Sioux War of 1876.

George Armstrong Custer would lead over 700 men into a battlefield that was massively underestimated. Over 260 of his men were killed and Custer himself would succumb to this horrible error in judgment.

The Dark Treasure of Little Bighorn

An artists rendition of the horrific battlefield

A lot has been written about this conflict, and a lot of people believe the truth has been covered up by the American government. Since there were so many high ranking casualties, much of the battle remains a mystery.

After the battle ended, army officials tried to examine the battle site. What they found baffled them. There were no dead Indians to be found anywhere, but there were plenty of American soldier bodies to be found.

Dead horses were piled high in makeshift walls. This was a last ditch effort to offer protection from the Indian tribes. Many of the American soldier's bodies could not be identified. Their bodies were stripped of all their clothing and ritually mutilated. The army scouts were forced to bury the bodies where they were found.

Custer's body was recovered with two gunshot wounds. One shot wound was in his left chest and the other was in his left temple. Some sources say he died as a direct result of the chest wound, while others say he shot himself to prevent capture.

The entire battle was said to only last 30 minutes to an hour. Native Indian accounts of the battle state that the Cheyenne and Sioux warriors simply overwhelmed the troops in one huge charge.

The Dark Treasure of Little Bighorn

Today, the entire site of the battlefield is a National Monument. It is protected and of course metal detecting the battlefield is out of the question, but in May of 1984 an archaeological group armed with metal detectors set out to discover what really happened during this bloody battle. I don't know about you, but I don't know if I would want to dig up anything at a site like this.

The Dark Treasure of Little Bighorn

Image courtesy of 1025wil
Here is what Last Stand Hill looks like today

The dig proved to be very helpful. Over 600 artifacts were discovered during the initial searches. Most of the artifacts were bullets, shells and slugs, but one woman found something a little on the creepy side.

Her metal detector made a promising signal. The signal meant there was a piece of gold directly under her coil. She quickly recovered the object. It was a ring, but there was something inside the ring. In the middle of the ring was a finger bone that belonged to the ring's owner.

Once the bloody battle was over, squaws from the main Indian camp were sent to the battlefield where they hunted down the mortally wounded soldiers. The remaining soldiers suffered greatly at the hands of the squaws. The Indian squaws were known to slowly torture the survivors. One of their preferred methods of torture was cutting off a soldier's fingers one at a time.

Yes, I can easily say that I would not want to be the person who recovered that ring with the finger bone still attached!

I could not obtain rights to a picture of this horrid find, but it can be found on the Internet if you want to do a little searching yourself.

Isle Haute

In the early 1700s, piracy was in full swing. Ships sailing with any sort of wealth were fair game, and many a ship was destroyed in the name of greed and gold. There are plenty of pirate legends out there, but one pirate by the name of Captain Edward Low just might be one of the craziest pirates that ever lived. Sociopath and psycho might as well have been this guy's middle names. He was nuts, and he liked to brutally murder anyone in his path.

Captain Ed started his pirate days at the bottom of the rung when he and twelve other crew members were cast aside after a failed mutiny attempt. Ed tried to shoot his commanding officer in the face, but somehow missed. Not a very good way to start off as a pirate is it?

Ed and his entire crew were set adrift in the ocean with no food and water. This was basically a death sentence, but Captain Ed and his crew of 12 managed to capture an entire ship, kill the captain and take over. This was Ed's first taste of piracy success. He liked what he was doing and it was not long until he had created quite a nasty reputation for himself. I won't even list the things he did to people in this book. His atrocities were sick and evil.

During his years of pillaging and plundering any ship in his path, he amassed quite an amount of treasure. Like any good pirate, Ed needed a place to hide his treasure. The hiding place would have to be the closest thing to hell on earth, and he found it in a little island located in the Bay of Fundy. The island was called Isle Haute.

The shore of this spit of land was only accessible a couple hours each day. The island had a vicious tide cycle where the water rose and fell over 50 feet with each tide change. These tidal movements are said to be the strongest in the entire world.

To make things even worse, this little island had cliffs over 300 feet tall and a thick population of over 30 different spider species. This was not the average spider hanging in the corner type of population. This was the ground crunching underneath your feet as you walked on spider after spider population. This is an island that time forgot.

Isle Haute

This sounded like the perfect place for mean old Captain Ed to hide his vast amounts of loot.

Captain Ed was successful at hiding his gold on the island, but he was never successful at retrieving it. Eventually he was captured and hung for his crimes of the high seas. His unclaimed treasure was said to be haunted by his ghost, but there were other possible ghostly apparitions that inhabited Isle Haute as well.

The island is also the location of a rather brutal murder by the evil Captain. Legend says that he beheaded an unruly crew member on the island. There have been several eyewitness reports of a headless ghost haunting the island made by various lighthouse keepers who were unfortunate enough to spend any length of time on this creepy island. Does this sound like a place you would like to metal detect? Wait, there is more!

An area of the island has been nicknamed Indian Flat. This area was named after an Indian woman who died of starvation.

So let's look at this island from a scary standpoint.

- 50 foot tidal surges.
- 300 feet rock cliffs.
- A spider population large enough to give anyone a severe case of arachnophobia.

- A Indian woman died of starvation on the island.
- A person was beheaded on the island and his headless ghost has been seen multiple times by multiple people.
- It was the location where one of the most notoriously brutal pirates to ever sail the seven seas buried his treasure.
- Said pirate never recovered his treasure and now his ghost haunts the island.

There are two ways of looking at these things. You could choose to believe all of these horrid facts and steer clear of the island, or you could look at it a little differently. Maybe all of these stories are really just stories. Maybe these stories were created to keep people away from the vast amounts of gold buried on the island. What better way to keep people away from your treasure than by creating some really believable frightening stories.

An adventurer by the name of Edward Rowe Snow chose the latter. He chose to pursue the treasure when he got his hands on an old treasure map that he believed led to the location of Captain Edward's secret stash.

In 1947, Edward Rowe Snow purchased a treasure map. The map was analyzed by experts who said the map was drawn on 17th century paper. It took Mr. Snow 7 years to get his hands on this map, and it took him another 5 years to decipher it. His old treasure map pointed right towards

Isle Haute

Isle Haute.

Snow managed to get his hands on a very early model metal detector. It was not something that you or I would have used. It was used by plumbers to help them locate pipes, but it would prove to be good enough for Snow.

When Snow arrived on the island, the lighthouse keeper told him that he was not the first person to come searching for treasure, but like any good treasure hunter Snow did not let this stop him.

The day was growing shorter when Snow started his search. He was using his metal detector near a hole a looter had previously uncovered when his detector alerted him to possible treasure. Snow looked over his shoulder at the setting sun and started digging in the already deep hole with his pickaxe. For 20 minutes he managed to carve out a deep hole.

As the sun sank below the horizon, Snow's pickaxe became snagged in the ground. He pulled and struggled until a human ribcage protruded from the side of the hole. Snow kept digging and on his next swing recovered more than he wanted. His pick caught something in the darkness. Once again he pulled. This time a human skull rolled out of the earth and across his feet where it came to a stop. The skull was staring right at him! This proved to be enough for Mr. Snow as he scrambled out of the pit in the weak light of the setting sun.

Isle Haute

Snow returned the next morning to finish his dig. He managed to uncover a total of eight gold coins that were over 200 years old. Initially Snow was not allowed to take the coins with him, but he eventually obtained an export license that allowed him to claim the gold

This could not have been all of Captain Ed's buried treasure. Perhaps it all still remains buried on Isle Haute. Let me know if you find it!

Ancient Indian Burial Mounds

Indian burial grounds have been part of American folklore for many years. People in Hollywood have cashed in on some of these stories with horror movies like House and Poltergeist. In these movies, homes were built on top of ancient Indian burial grounds and as a result, the houses were haunted. These might be Hollywood movie stories, but who in their right mind would want to disturb any sort of burial grounds, let alone an Indian burial site.

Most people would choose to not willingly tamper with any type of grave site. Never mind the possibility of ghosts and poltergeists. It has to do with respect, but that has not stopped people from accidentally uncovering graves with a metal detector.

There are countless unmarked Indian burial sites across the United States. There really is no way of knowing you are about to dig one up until it is too late. This still doesn't make matters any better for the unfortunate person who accidentally uncovers a grave.

Eventually someone is going to find an old Indian burial ground, and that is exactly what Ray Camp did on December 15th 2013.

Ray stumbled upon his find on accident. He had no intentions on finding anything. He was simply testing out a metal detector near his house. Ray is a member of the Alabama Archeometalology Historical Society and the members of this society often receive new metal detectors for testing purposes. The members of this society are no strangers to metal detecting. Some of the founding members have been avid treasure hunters for over 40 years, and they have made some pretty incredible finds over those 40 years, but let's get back to the point at hand: Indian burial grounds.

All of this happened in a small town in Alabama by the name of Wetumpka.

Ray was testing out this metal detector when he got a good signal. Not expecting to find much, Ray started to recover the target. To his surprise, he unearthed a couple of copper bracelets. As he tried to recover the bracelets, Ray got yet another surprise. The bracelets were still attached to bones. Arm bones to be exact.

At this point Ray decided he had better stop the recovery. He made a few phone calls and decided to call the local law enforcement. He wanted to make sure he did not stumble upon a crime scene.

Once the local law authorities declared that the area was not a crime scene, a team of state archeologists were called in to survey the area and remove any other remaining artifacts.

Ancient Indian Burial Mounds

Several bones were recovered along with some beads and a few human teeth. Ray and other members of the Alabama Archeometalology Historical Society have been quoted saying, "This is the find of a lifetime!"

This might be the find of a lifetime, but I don't think I would like to be the one who made this discovery. You can call me superstitious. You can call me silly and you can call me a chicken. I would much rather be a silly superstitious guy in a chicken suit than dig up an Indian burial site. Let's just hope that no Hollywood type ghost stories rise from this possible Indian burial mound.

Child Coffin

On April 7th 2010, Ken Mordle was having a great time during an organized metal detecting exhibition. The exhibition was organized by a metal detecting club called: Digging Up the Past Metal Detecting Club. The club and its lucky members organize routine digs on the English countryside. This particular dig was taking place near Chichester West Sussex, UK.

Ken was happily hunting an area when his metal detector signaled treasure. Ken started digging up his find. Thoughts of old hoards raced through his head. Could he have just stumbled upon the next big Roman hoard? Would his find go down in the history books? It definitely would, but he did not find the next big Roman hoard.

He found a coffin. This was not just any coffin either. It was the coffin of a Roman child that was over 1900 years old. The entire coffin and its contents were removed by a team of archeologists for further study.

Child Coffin

A team of four archeologists painstakingly combed through the remains looking for any clues to help them identify the find. The first attempt involved a camera being pushed down into the coffin. They quickly learned the entire coffin was filled with silt. This meant they would have to remove the silt very slowly while analyzing every tiny speck.

Their work revealed bones, small bracelets and one small bead. The coffin belonged to a little girl, but it was the only coffin found in the area. Why was she buried here all alone? It is this question that makes the story a little more interesting. The question remains unanswered.

Once the find was made public, people were allowed to

Child Coffin

vote on a name for the little girl. The name that was chosen is Oriens. This word comes from the Latin verb which means "to rise." I hope this little girl's spirit does not live up to her newly appointed name.

The Thetford Hoard

They always say that you should leave the best for last, and this particular metal detecting story is the best or worst depending on how you look at things. Crematory tags, rings with fingers attached, Indian burial sites and coffins with the remains of children don't even come close to the supernatural qualities of this find. If you found any of the prior finds even the slightest bit frightening, then hold on tight because this one makes a 5 star Hollywood horror film seem like a nice cozy children's bedtime story.

Arthur Brooks was the star of this find. Notice how I did not say he was the "lucky" one here? You should also notice that I am speaking of Arthur in the past tense because he is no longer among the living. His death and this find have been the centerpiece of controversy and hushed debates at many a pub over frothy mugs of ale.

Some say he died as a direct result of this find and the pieces of the hoard are cursed. Others say it was just coincidence. I will let you be the judge. Here is what happened in November of 1979.

Arthur Brooks was illegally searching some land that was scheduled to be built upon when he found the hoard. He did not have permission to hunt and knowing that the area would no longer be accessible, he quickly scrambled to retrieve as much of the hoard as possible before it got too

The Thetford Hoard

dark.

Arthur kept his find hidden for six months before deciding to sell it on the black market. Once the pieces started arriving on the black market, archeological investigators started to track it down.

By the time they figured everything out, Arthur was terminally Ill. He died in July of 1980 less than 8 months after making the find. Of those 8 months, Arthur kept the treasure in his possession for six.

The original dig site could no longer be accessed because a building has been built on top of it. We will never know the true entire contents of the hoard, but we do know Arthur recovered the following items.

- 23 high purity gold rings
- 3 silver strainers
- 33 silver spoons
- 4 gold bracelets
- 5 gold necklaces or neck chains
- 4 necklace pendants
- 2 sets of necklace clasps
- 1 gold amulet filled with sulfur
- 5 beads – 1 emerald, 1 engraved, 3 glass
- 1 gold belt buckle
- 1 shale box

The Thetford Hoard

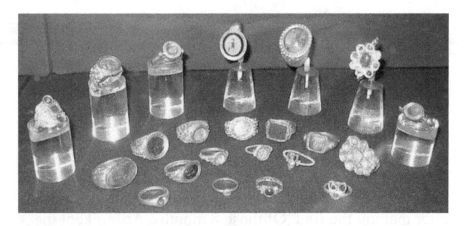

What's so scary about all of these great finds? It looks like beautiful jewelry doesn't it? These are the types of things everyone with a metal detector wants to uncover, but some people believe these items were cursed. Here is why.

The gold amulet filled with sulfur is the first clue. Sulfur has often been associated with demons, ghost stories and hell itself. Why would there be a gold amulet filled with sulfur buried with all of these seemingly harmless pieces of treasure?

Many of the rings in this hoard appear in near perfect condition. These rings are made of a high purity gold. Some of them are 94% gold. There is a reason why modern jewelry is not made from pure gold like this. It has nothing to do with prices.

Gold in pure form is soft. It is so soft that rings made from high purity gold often bend or break after being worn for a very short time. None of the rings in this hoard appear to have ever been worn. How could rings that are over 400 years old and made from almost pure gold be in near perfect condition? They shouldn't be.

Many of the rings in this hoard have other worldly inscriptions that are said to invoke demons. One specific ring that depicts a snake legged deity is inscribed with "a powerful magic word" that is often associated with demons. This word does not belong to any known human language, but instead this word is said to be the language that only demons can understand. Creepsville!

The only person who knows the true circumstances surrounding this hoard is Arthur, and we all know what happened to him shortly after retrieving this hoard. He became terminally ill and died. Is the Thetford hoard cursed? You can find out for yourself. Parts of the hoard, including the rings with demonic inscriptions are currently on display at the British Museum. I think I will pass on visiting this exhibit! No thanks!

Incredible Metal Detecting Finds Made by Kids!

Enough of the dark supernatural finds. Let's travel to the opposite end of the spectrum and talk about something bright and shiny. I am not talking about gold. I am talking about kids!

Metal detecting is a great hobby for kids. It gets them outside and in the sun. It also teaches them valuable history lessons. I think everyone will agree that most children today spend far too much time indoors. Getting them outside can be a challenge. What can we do about it? We can introduce them to the best hobby in the world: metal detecting.

What kid doesn't love the idea of digging up some treasure? I don't know about you, but I spent many an afternoon as a kid day dreaming of some long lost treasure. It wasn't until later that I actually started finding it. I have made quite a few great memories on my own, but some of my favorites involve hunting with my kids. The first story in this part of the book is a personal favorite. I learned a very important lesson that day. Here is what happened.

Shells On the Beach

When my son goes metal detecting with me, he likes to do all of the digging. He demands it now, so I let him do all of the work.

I have been teaching him how to use the scoop, and how to identify and find items in that scoop of sand. You may not believe this, but sometimes it can be hard to see your treasure in that small amount of sand. Coins like to stay hidden, and they are harder to see to the untrained eye.

I decided to take my son on a real adventure. He loves to explore, so I asked him if he wanted to metal detect an old island, one that had most likely never been detected. He only had one thing to say, "When?"

We left that day. We had to take a boat to get to the island, and at the front of the island was a small exposed beach. This would be the place to check first. People frequent the island, and they are always right on this small strip of beach.

We hit the beach and started getting signals immediately. They were only 1-2 feet apart, and some were within inches of each other. We were finding a lot of fishing tackle, and a lot of older clad coins. We were also finding some really interesting things that we could not identify. They were small discs that looked like they could be really old coins.

We both glanced at these things, threw them in our stash, and kept hunting. It had already been a couple of hours, and we were almost done with this tiny stretch of beach. It was hard to believe that two hours had already gone by.

I got a big signal, and I mean big as in size. It sounded like a can. It was too big to be anything else. I told my son, "Hey, there is a big target here, but I would just leave it. It is a can."

He grabbed the scoop, and started digging. I shook my head and started searching the beach again. A few seconds later I hear him scream. It was a good scream. I turn around and he yells dad, "It is a huge sniper bullet." In his hands was an unfired .50 caliber round. It was huge, and I thought to myself, "Could he have possibly fired this thing if he hit it with the scoop just right?" I suddenly did not want him to dig any more targets.

He was holding a very old .50 caliber bullet, and he was thrilled. He looked at me and said, "Good thing I decided to dig up that can, huh dad?" Smart-ass! This was one of mine, and one of his best finds. Here is a picture of that old shell.

Shells On the Beach

On that day I learned a couple of very valuable things.

1. There is live ammo out there.
2. Never assume a target is garbage until you dig it up.

I have since made even more great memories treasure hunting with my son. My daughter has now caught the treasure hunting bug and she is always eager to go out for a hunt.

Boom! Boom!

There have been so many wars and battles on our planet that many metal detecting enthusiasts actively seek out old war relics. These types of relics can be easy targets because they are so abundant, but these are not the types of treasure that most kids actively search for. In fact, most kids don't know war relics when they see them. Such is the case with these two amazing finds!

7 Year old Sonny Carter from King's Lynn was busy opening his morning Christmas presents. To his surprise, one of them happened to be a metal detector. Sonny's parents thought he would be finding some spare change here and there, but they had no idea what he would come home with on his very first outing.

Sonny and his older brother Marley decided to try the metal detector in their garden. It did not take them long to locate their first target. Eagerly, the two boys started digging up what they thought was a treasure chest full of gold. What they got instead was a large mud covered rusty piece of iron.

The two boys took their prized find inside to show their dad Jem. The excitement of the find spread through the house like a wild brush fire. Jem started cleaning the mud away from the find. Within a few seconds, Jem knew that what he was holding in his bare hands was not made from

Boom! Boom!

gold. It was an old World War II era bomb. Jem quickly phoned the authorities.

The authorities told Jem to place the bomb in a bucket of water. Because of their location, the authorities were concerned that they may have uncovered an old German phosphorous bomb. These bombs were nasty business and they were designed to detonate when they dried out. One phosphorous bomb would release a white hot wall of flame. Maybe this story should have been under the frightening section of this book?

The police and the bomb squad showed up at the house to take care of the bomb. As it turns out, the bomb was not armed. It was simply a practice bomb that was used for training purposes. Needless to say, I think I would have needed to change my pants if my son walked in the door with an old World War II bomb.

A couple of kids in Folkestone England had a similar experience in January of 2014. Kane Byrne and his buddy Alex Taylor were busy exploring on their day off from school. They were outside looking for buried treasures with a metal detector.

They unearthed what looked like a large metal bottle of some sort. The two boys brought their find home and gave it a good cleaning. They still had no idea what they had found, but they decided to go back and look for more.

Boom! Boom!

To their surprise, there was another large metal looking bottle object buried right next to the first one. Once again the two boys brought the item home and immediately went to work cleaning it.

Kayne was eager to show his father what he and Alex had uncovered. Kayne's father Karl tried not to panic when he realized that the two boys had unearthed two World War II anti tank shells. If these shells detonated, nothing in a 6 foot radius would remain but smoldering ashes.

This is where this particular story differs from the first. These two World War II shells were not practice shells. They were actual live shells that could have exploded at any minute. Maybe this story should have been located under the frightening section as well. Luckily no one was hurt. The two shells were disarmed by the local police and the bomb squad.

Civil War Relic History Lesson

Seven year old Lucas Hall from Clarke County Virginia has decided to show us all up by making an amazing find within his first week of metal detecting. It seems young Lucas became very interested in metal detecting after speaking with a neighbor who was a seasoned relic hunter. His neighbor was even nice enough to give Lucas a few choice Civil War bullets. That was it. Lucas was hooked before he even got a chance to swing a coil.

When his 7th birthday rolled around, what do you think young Lucas asked for? He did not ask for an Xbox. He wanted a metal detector. His parents made his dream come true by giving Lucas a Garret Ace 150 and it didn't take Lucas long to start recovering some of his own relics.

Lucas, along with his sister and his father set out to find some real Civil War treasures on private property. The area surrounding Lucas's home is rich in Civil War history. There were six epic battles in his hometown alone. It did not take them long to start locating plenty of relics. Some of the relics were quite obvious, while others were not. Lucas held on to all of them.

One Saturday afternoon, Lucas and his dad set off on 4 wheelers looking for a new place to hunt. Lucas saw a spot that looked good to him and they started hunting. It did not take Lucas long to locate a good sized target in the ground.

Civil War Relic History Lesson

His dad told him that because of the size, it was most likely an old fence post or something.

Lucas was determined and he kept digging. Together the two of them unearthed a once in a lifetime Civil War relic. It was a Civil War sabre! Lucas and his father could not have been happier with their new discovery.

Lucas and his older sister are both homeschooled. His mother has created history lessons from all of their finds. On a recent trip to a Civil War museum, Lucas and his sister were able to identify some more of the items they uncovered. Each item has taught them a little piece of history. Now Lucas and his sister are learning from every single relic they recover.

It did not take long for news of the great Civil War sabre find to spread. Garrett, the company who manufactures the machine young Lucas was using caught wind of the find. They sent him a new metal detector that was a step up from his current one. Lucas plans on giving his old metal detector to his sister so the two of them can hunt together.

This is one great metal detecting story that has taught valuable history lessons and brought the entire family together. Congratulations Lucas. You deserve it.

Space Treasure

There are different types of treasure out there. Some of us eagerly look for old coins. Some of us get bitten by the gold bug. Some of us look for old relics that help rewrite history and some of us hunt for space treasure. This space treasure comes in the form of meteorites. Some scientists even believe this is how gold arrived on our planet, in the form of meteorites.

Meteorite hunting, just like any other form of metal detecting can become quite addictive. How often do you get to hold a 10,000 year old rock from outer space in your hands? For most of us this opportunity never arrives, but that was not the case for Jansen Lyons.

Jansen, a 13 year old homeschooled boy became very interested in meteorites after reading a book that explained them in great detail. The book captured his imagination and he started examining every single rock he could get his hands on.

Seeing his determination, Jansen's grandfather designed and built the boy a metal detector. You read that right. His grandfather did not go out to the store and purchase a metal detector. He built his own for his grandson. How cool is that?

Jansen quickly went to work using his homemade metal

detector and in September of 2011 he came across what he thought was a two pound hunk of space treasure. The only problem was that Jansen had no way of identifying or authenticating his find. It sat in his room for a year before he got scientific proof.

Jansen and his mother learned that the University of New Mexico had a museum of meteorites, but the museum was closed for months while a new security system was being installed. It seems that someone broke into the museum and stole a very high profile meteorite that was worth a large sum of money. Go figure. Thieves are everywhere.

Once the museum reopened, Jansen and his mother were granted a private tour. Jansen brought his space rock with him. He was eager to show it off and find out what it was. Their tour guide was convinced Jansen was carrying around a two pound rock. It was nothing special and it definitely was no meteorite.

Meteorites are very rare, and one of this size has never been found in his home town of Rio Rancho. It could not possibly be anything but your average New Mexico rock, but Jansen insisted that his rock was no ordinary rock.

Finally, the museum agreed to test his find. It would take the museum a few hours to determine what the rock was so Jansen and his mother went home where they waited for the phone call.

Space Treasure

When the phone rang, the house fell silent while the news was delivered. His ordinary rock was no ordinary rock at all. It was an L6 ordinary chondrite. A rare meteorite and it was over 10,000 years old. Jansen has agreed to put a small sample of his two pound space treasure on display at the New Mexico Museum.

Jansen's story is not one of beginner's luck, but one of hard work, determination and passion. This is something that every single one of us can learn from.

Can you believe he found his monster two pound meteorite with a homemade metal detector? It just shows that hard work and determination are well rewarded. Awesome!

Beginner's Luck

Jansen Lyons proved that hard work and dedication are always rewarded, but there is such a thing as beginner's luck, and that is exactly what three year old James Hyatt experienced on his very first metal detecting outing with his father. His incredible find has become the envy of many people. Here are the details.

Sunday, May 17th 2009 was an epic day for young James. James and his father were searching for adventure using an entry level metal detector when the machine gave them a good signal. They were searching a field in Hockley, Essex England.

The two started to recover the find when the dad saw a glimmer of gold in the bottom of the hole. Their treasure was buried a measly six or eight inches down, but it would turn out to be the find of a lifetime.

Image courtesy of Portable Antiquities Scheme

When they finally recovered the treasure, they knew it was gold, but they had no idea the age or value of the item. It

Page 135

would be a year before they found out what they had uncovered.

They had unearthed a gold pendant from the first half of the 16th century. The front of the pendant was engraved with a picture of a female saint holding a cross. This image is believed to be the Virgin Mary.

The back of the pendant slides open to reveal a cavity, but it was damaged and could not be opened. It is believed the pendant was designed to hold a religious relic.

Curators at the British Museum created a special probe and used a microscope to repair and remove the damaged rear lid. It now opens and closes along the grooves cut into the side panel.

Inside the pendant, researchers found matted root hairs and small outer stems of unprocessed flax. It is believed these were pieces of locally grown flax plants.

Three sides of the pendant were engraved with the names of the three wise men and the fourth side was engraved with leaves. What a magnificent piece of history. The estimated value of this find is: £2,500,000 or $4,100,000.

Wouldn't it be great to uncover something like this with your children? There is no reason why you can't. Get out there and have some fun metal detecting with your kids. You could find something even better.

Incredible Ring Finds

Sooner or later every person with a metal detector will find a ring. Hopefully it is not a cursed demon ring like the rings of the Thetford Hoard and hopefully is not the demonic ring from The Lord of the Rings movies. *My Precious!* Although it may be a copy of that infamous ring. I did find one on a playground once. It fit perfectly on my finger and the world went dark when I put it on. Then I noticed the gold plating peeling away from the side and my little daydream was shattered. Oh well, off to the next target.

Rings are a somewhat common find. Beach hunters are lucky enough to dig up hundreds of them every year. They may be made of platinum, silver or gold and they may be covered in jewels. They may also be nothing but costume jewelry. Either way, finding a ring is a great experience. It doesn't matter if you are waist deep in the water and you get a glint of gold in the bottom of your beach scoop, or if you remove a freshly cut plug and spy a hint of silver peeking out from the dirt. Rings are on the top of the "gotta find" list of almost every single person wildly swinging a metal detector.

Rings have been used by people for over 6000 years. Most rings are used as symbols. The circle means infinity. It goes on forever and that is why rings are used as a symbol of marriage. They symbolize one person's never ending love for another. Cue the romantic music and dim the lights. Here are some of the most incredible metal detecting ring finds!

I have been fortunate enough to find several rings on my metal detecting adventures. It is something that I never seem to grow tired of. The next two ring stories are my own personal stories. They are from my book entitled: Metal Detecting the Beach. Enjoy.

A Big Ring and a UFO

When Summer rolls around, I prefer to hunt the beach right before the sun goes down and continue after the sun has set. It can be exhilarating to be on the beach on a clear Summer night. A nice breeze to keep things cool, and plenty of things to dig up in the dark.

I remember one evening in the middle of the Summer when two strange things happened to me. I was walking North along the beach and my plan was to hunt where everyone had parked on my way up the beach, and then when I turned to come back, I would work the low tide line. According to the local weather reports, it was going to be a perfect night.

By the time I was halfway through my hunt, I had already found two nice gold rings where people had been parking their cars. I was in great spirits and the sun was setting. Soon I would have the beach to myself.

The sun went down, and the stars lit the sky. It was beautiful. I was getting tired so I decided it was time to turn and head back. I could hit the low tide zone and keep my feet wet.

I approached the low tide line eagerly, and that's when I saw it. It was a shooting star. I was lucky to see such a good one, and then out of the corner of my eye, it flew back up into the sky. What the heck was that? I had never seen anything like it. There it was again and this time it fell again just below the horizon, and a few seconds later it rose back out of sight. I was baffled, but It looked like I was getting closer to this mysterious object in the night sky.

It would fall out of the sky and then shoot back up like a rocket. It was just barely visible. I was watching the sky, and suddenly my metal detector made a sound that I loved to hear. It was a nice tone that 4 out of ten times meant gold was buried under my coil. I dug a quick scoop and looked over my shoulder and the UFO was still doing its crazy dance through the sky.

I threw the scoop of sand on the dry beach and moved my coil over the hole I had just dug. No more target. I had retrieved it in that scoop of sand. It was dark, and I had to feel my way through the pile of sand. I stuck my hand in the sand pile and a ring slid right around my finger. I laughed out loud.

I pulled my hand out of the sand pile and reached down with my other hand to try and feel the ring that was around my finger. I could not see anything. My thumb brushed the top of the ring, and my heart raced. There was a huge setting on top of the ring. If this thing was a diamond, it was a big one.

I don't carry a light with me when I hunt at night, but I do

carry a cell phone. I quickly
fumbled for my cell phone so that I could shed some light
on my recent find.

The light that came from the cell phone was just enough
light to tease me even more. I was still a good distance
from my car. I kept the ring on my finger, and looked back
at the UFO. It was still there. I started to walk faster
towards where I had parked my car.

As I got closer to my car, I got closer to the UFO. It was
not that far out there. I squinted to try and make sense of it,
and then it hit me. It was a kite. I could see the kite string
in the moonlight. I followed the string to a gazebo on the
beach. Someone had tied this kite to the top of the gazebo
and it was flying up and down all on its own. For a while it
had me stumped.

When I got home, I told my wife, "I think I found a huge
diamond ring." Her response was, "Let me see it." I held
out my hand, and she slid the ring off my pinky finger.
I could see it in the light, and it was huge! I handed her the
jewelers loupe so she could look for any markings.

There was a 14k stamp on the inside of the ring. A quick
acid test told us that the ring was real 14k gold, but what
about the diamond? I did not have a diamond tester, so I
would have to wait until morning to take it to a
professional who instantly verified that it was indeed a real
diamond. It was just over 1 carat in size. How would you

A Big Ring and a UFO

like to find something like this?

Don't Throw Anything Away

It may seem like junk at first, but you should never ever throw anything away that you find unless you are 100% positive that it is garbage. There are instances of people throwing away old Spanish coins because they just looked like large black metal discs. A quick flick of the wrist, and those 300 year old coins skip right across the water where they quickly sink to the bottom waiting to be found by someone with a little more experience. It may be an object of mystery now, but in the future you may be able to figure out exactly what it is. I have the perfect example.

I was hunting a section of beach during the early morning hours. The beach that I was hunting allows driving. People drive up and down the beach all day long. The night before, there was a huge Mardis Gras parade that went down the beach. There were thousands of people everywhere. Now you know why I wanted to hunt the area the next morning.

A large crowd of partying people leave one thing behind, and they leave it behind in huge numbers. Trash. It was everywhere. It was rather disgusting actually. Empty beer bottles and cans right next to garbage cans.

I was finding plenty of bottle tops, pull tabs, and other miscellaneous pieces of garbage. It was hard work, but I was cleaning up the beach, and the beach likes to reward

Don't Throw Anything Away

you every once in a while. I got a good low tone on my
metal detector. It was right in the middle of a tire track,
and it was a shallow target.

I was hunting the dry. I quickly sifted the sand through my
scoop, and in the bottom of my scoop was a smashed ring.
At least I thought it was a ring. It must have been some
cheap costume jewelry from the Mardis Gras parade. I put
it in my pocket and went on hunting. Here is a picture of
the smashed ring.

When I got home, I showed the crushed ring to my wife,
and she said the same thing. "It looks like costume jewelry

Don't Throw Anything Away

from the parade. I tossed it in my pile of junk jewelry that I kept in an old tackle box, and completely forgot about it. At the time I had no idea how to acid test a piece of jewelry, so that smashed ring sat in my tackle box for over a year.

A year passed and in that year, I learned a lot about how to identify jewelry. I had purchased an acid test and a jewelers loupe, and I had become very good at Iding my finds.

I got back from a recent hunt where I found some junk jewelry. I keep everything and you should too. I tossed my new junk jewelry into my pile that was growing in my tackle box and that smashed ring bounced to the top of the pile. I had completely forgotten about it. I realized that I had never looked at it with a loupe or anything.

I quickly grabbed the smashed ring from the pile and looked at it with my loupe. A large part of the band was missing, and there were no markings. I showed it to my wife and told her to take a look. She looked at it, and then she flipped it around and looked at all
of the stones on the front. Then she says this to me, "The top of this ring is all smashed and broken, but the stones don't have a scratch on them. Do you think they could be real diamonds?" The thought had never crossed my mind. It was just costume jewelry.

I wanted to try a diamond test that I had learned about.

Don't Throw Anything Away

Sometimes, but not all of the times, a diamond will glow a milky white if you put it under a black light. My son had a black light in his room. I flipped the light on, and three of the stones had that strange glow. I was convinced they were real diamonds which meant that the ring was either white gold or platinum.

I broke out the acid test and it tested as 18k gold. I was thrilled. This ring had quite a few large diamonds in it. I took it to a jeweler to have it looked at. As soon as I handed it to him he tossed it up in the air a few times and said, "This is platinum." He looked at the stones and said, "All of the stones are real, and they are very old.

They are a very old style diamond called European Mine cut. This ring is from the early 1900s or even earlier." I was thrilled to say the least. I asked him if he could repair it, and he said "Of Course!" Within a few days it was repaired and on my wife's finger.

When I first found this ring, I had almost thrown it in the garbage. Just think about that for a second. I had an antique platinum diamond ring that had over 2 carats of diamonds in it sitting in my house for over a year, and I had no idea. DON'T THROW ANYTHING AWAY!

Don't Throw Anything Away

Long Lost Ring

In 1934, B. M. Chumbley graduated from his local Draper high school class. Like many other proud graduates, Chumbley got a class ring to signify his huge accomplishment. He made it through a huge chapter in his life.

His class ring was made from 10 karat gold and adorned with a beautiful blue stone. The outside of the ring had intricate detailing and on the inside were his initials.

About a month later Chumbley and a group of friends went swimming at a local creek. This is when Chumbley noticed his class ring was missing. He assumed it came off while swimming in the creek. It wouldn't be the first time a person lost a ring while swimming. It happens all the time, but this was not where he lost his ring.

Let's hop in a time machine and travel 79 years into the future. Chumbley is now 97 years old and that old class ring is nothing more than some far off memory. Chumbley still resides in the same city. He even still lives in the same house as the day he graduated high school.

He gets a knock on his door. A man by the name of Robert O'neal is standing at his door. Robert, a retired Virginia probation - parole officer and avid metal detecting enthusiast asks Chumbley if he can have permission to

Long Lost Ring

metal detect his property.

Robert is ready to put his Minelab E-trac to good work. Robert knows the property is old and it may hide some older coins.

Chumbley gives Robert permission and the hunt is on. Robert's first target is a penny. Nothing worth mentioning. His next target reveals a glimpse of gold in the soil. Robert gets excited and plucks a gold ring from the ground. He continues his hunt and manages to squeeze out a few more choice coins before calling it the day.

When Robert gets home, he decides to give the gold ring he found a good cleaning. Washing away the caked on soil reveals an inscription that reads 1934 BMC. Robert realizes what the inscription means and a month later returns to Chumbley's house.

Robert asks Mr. Chumbley if he ever lost anything, specifically a ring. Chumbley tells Robert about how he lost his class ring so long ago. Smiling, Robert pulls the old class ring from his pocket and hands it to Chumbley. Chumbley was excited to have his long lost ring back in his hands. These are the types of metal detecting stories that make digging through all the trash worthwhile.

42 Years In the Ground

In 1956, William Reeve married the love of his life. Her name was Marion. A gold wedding band that fit perfectly on Marion's finger became a symbol of their marriage. They were madly in love and together they had three wonderful children.

In 1971, 15 years after they were married, Marion was hanging the wash to dry when she noticed her wedding ring was no longer on her finger. It was as if the ring had vanished into thin air.

Of course Marion was upset about the loss of her gold wedding band and it was quickly replaced, but Marion longed for her original wedding ring. Over the years, her entire family searched for her missing ring. For decades they scoured the yard and garden looking for that ring, but it never did show up.

Chris Blackburn a metal detecting enthusiast approached the family seeking permission to search their property for coins. Chris's first hunt revealed a few coins here and there but nothing special.

Years later, Chris returns to hunt their property once again. Marion was upstairs watching Chris as he swung his trusty metal detector. She watched him recover something and make his way towards the house.

42 Years In the Ground

When Marion answered the door, Chris stood there with her long lost gold wedding ring in his hand. Marion, whose husband had died four years earlier became very emotional.

The ring was in excellent condition even though it had been buried just a few inches in the ground for 42 years. The entire family thanked Chris for returning the ring.

This story proves that metal detecting uncovers all kinds of treasures. For Chris, the treasure was seeing Marion's face when he handed her that long lost wedding band!

The Traveling Ring

Julie and her high school sweetheart Sam Simeon from Alaska were married. Sam picked out a small gold ring for Julie. The ring had two heart shaped stones. One was an emerald and the other was a topaz. Sam also had both of their names engraved along the inside of the band along with the phrase, "our love grows stronger." The ring was all the two young lovebirds could afford.

The two newlyweds were vacationing with the groom's parents in Hawaii. What do you do while you are in Hawaii? You swim. Who could say no to some of the most beautiful waters in the world? Julie couldn't and it was not long until her wedding ring slipped right off her finger and sank in the sand below.

Frantically the two newlyweds searched for the ring using snorkeling equipment. The ring didn't show up. Was the loss of the ring an omen? Was it a sign that they were married too young? Julie refused to believe it.

A week later, the father of the groom ran into a local lifeguard who was metal detecting. He told the lifeguard about his daughter in law's recent loss. The lifeguard scoured the beach looking for the ring, but the ring still did not turn up. Out of time, the entire family had to return to their home state of Alaska without the ring.

The Traveling Ring

A few days passed and the lifeguard ran into another metal detecting buddy who just so happened to be accompanied by his twin brother. Can you guess where the twin brother was from? He was from Alaska.

The lifeguard and his friend started talking about the ring when his friend exclaimed he found that same ring a few days ago buried under 10 inches or more of sand! Now they just needed to get the ring back home to Alaska. Well how convenient is it that the man who found the ring had a twin brother who was visiting from Alaska? They were able to get in touch with the newlywed's father in law and when the twin returned home to Alaska, he brought the ring with him.

Sam, the new groom decided to surprise his wife with the returned ring. He wrapped it and put it under their Christmas tree. What a great Christmas present!

Imagine the journey that ring went through. It slid off her finger and quickly sank in the sand, where it was recovered by a metal detecting enthusiast who had a twin brother from Alaska, who would bring the ring back with him over 3000 miles to be returned to its rightful owner! What are the odds? Incredible!

Surprise Ring

Rings are almost always a surprise, but John Hill uncovered one heck of a surprise ring while metal detecting with his three grandchildren on some private farmland in Sampford Peverell, Mid-Devon, England.

John's metal detector alerted him to some possible buried treasure. He gathered his three grandchildren around to uncover the treasure. They eagerly dug down about 10 inches to reveal a shiny silver ring. Excitement filled the air. They had uncovered a real piece of treasure, but as John got a little closer to their newly uncovered ring, he looked up and told his grandchildren to run!

The ring he was staring at was the pull ring to a live grenade that was still buried in the earth. John quickly notified the local authorities who sent out the Royal Navy bomb disposal experts.

The entire area was fenced off and the Royal Navy bomb disposal experts quickly went to work setting a charge on the live grenade. The grenade was detonated and the explosion was heard from a mile away. Luckily, John and his grandchildren were all safe.

It is still uncertain how the grenade got there, but remains from a 1961 Canberra bomber were recently discovered nearby in a canal. It is possible the grenade came from the

Surprise Ring

cockpit of the old bomber.

It just goes to show that you never really know what you might be digging up, and it also teaches us the importance of a slow and steady recovery method. Had John been using a large shovel to recover this item, he would have pulled the ring and the attached pin never even knowing it until BOOM! Always be cautious when recovering what you might think is buried treasure.

17th Century Gold

Its not every day that you get to recover a 17th century gold mourning ring using a metal detector, but in June of 2010 that is exactly what Peter Amison did! Mourning rings were often worn during this century. They were worn in memory of a loved one who had recently passed away.

These rings were often made from gold and Jet, a black stone. On some mourning rings, a small lock of hair was placed under the stone. Some mourning rings even featured a portrait. The rings were also inscribed with the deceased person's name and date of death. Mourning rings were purchased before death and left in a will to surviving members of the family. Peter made his find in the Newcastle, England area.

Peter knew he had recovered a nice ring, but he had no idea the significance of the ring until after he spoke with an antique trader. The ring dates back to sometime between 1600 and 1700. The inscription inside the ring reads, "death has surprised my chiefest jewel." The ring is made from 10% gold.

As of this writing, the ring was being stored by the British Museum in London. It was not currently on display. There are a few museums currently trying to obtain the ring and put it on display. Think of the history behind that ring. What an incredible ring find.

The Raglan Ring

In 1998 a fellow by the name of Ron Treadgold made a discovery that would become part of history. His discovery was a ring, but it was not just any ordinary ring. The ring he found would be called the largest gold signet ring ever discovered, and he did it using nothing more than a metal detector.

This incredible ring find was near Raglan Castle, Monmouthshire, Wales in the UK.

Signet rings were used to make impressions in wax. This was how people sealed private letters and important documents. If the seal was broken, then it was quite obvious the item had been opened. The impression that was made into the wax also verified that the letter or document was coming from a high ranking official.

The face of the Raglan ring is designed with a lion on a bed of flowers. This would have been the impression that was left in the fresh wax. There is also an inscription around the lion that reads, "to yow feythfoul." Today this would translate to, "go get me a pizza." I am kidding of course. Today this would translate to, "faithful to you." On one side of the lion the letter W appears and on the other side the letter A appears. These letters would have also appeared on the wax seal.

The Raglan Ring

This large ring was obviously a man's ring, but the ring was so large that it would not fit on the average man's hand. It could have only fit on the hand of a giant. Historians believe this particular ring was so large because it would have been worn over a leather glove. Historians also believe this ring would have been used by an important officer, but they are not sure who.

The Raglan ring is very old. Historians believe the ring was made somewhere between 1440 and 1475. The ring is currently on display at The British Museum. It is on loan from the National Museums & Galleries of Wales.

You can see this impressive find yourself at the following web address:
http://www.britishmuseum.org/images/loan12077a_1.jpg

Could you imagine what it would have been like to discover this impressive ring?

The Escrick Ring

Michael Greenhorn did not plan on making history when he went metal detecting in a field near the village of Escrick, south of York, England, but that is exactly what he did in 2009.

This particular find is a ring, but it is a ring that is full of mystery. A team of over 30 archeologists and historians have gotten together to discuss the origins of his incredible find.

At first glance, the team determined the ring must have come from the early 10th or 11th century, but it appears that this ring is even older, possibly 600 years old. That would mean this ring was over 1600 years old. Think about that for just a second.

The Escrick ring is a beautiful ring made from gold. Its craftsmanship is unlike anything anyone has seen. It is approximately 1 inch (2.5 cm) across. It holds some beautiful glass and a magnificent large sapphire is mounted in the middle.

See this impressive work of art yourself at the following web address:
http://i.huffpost.com/gen/1062562/thumbs/o-ESCRICK-RING-570.jpg

The Escrick Ring

Who owned this ring over 1600 years ago? That is a question the group of historians and archeologists have been asking themselves. They initially thought this ring would have belonged to a bishop, but now they think this ring belonged to royalty, possibly even the king of France!

This is what metal detecting dreams are made of. Michael Greenhorn sold the ring to the Yorkshire Museum for just over $50,000 or £29,792. It looks like Michael paid for more than his metal detector with this incredible ring find.

These are just a handful of the incredible ring finds people are making every single day using nothing more than a metal detector.

The Newark Torc

Finding a ring is always nice, but could you imagine what it must be like to discover a ring that is big enough to go around a person's neck. I don't mean a necklace. I mean a torc, or as we would call it in modern times, a choker, Maurice Richardson knows exactly what it feels like.

Maurice was no newcomer to the hobby of metal detecting. He had been at it for about 40 years before he made this once in a lifetime discovery, and he was not using a new fancy machine either. He was using his old faithful metal detector that was over 30 years old.

In February of 2005, Maurice was searching in a field on the edge of Newark-on-Trent, Nottinghamshire, England. It was no picture perfect hunting day either. It was cold, wet and rainy, but that did not stop Maurice.

His trusty old metal detector alerted him to possible treasure and his initial thoughts were to leave it. It was raining far too hard and he was getting tired, but he just could not get the thought of possible treasure out of his mind. He had to dig it up. Who knows, it could be the find of a lifetime he thought.

He started to dig and dig and dig. Whatever it was, it was buried deep down in the earth. At two feet, Maurice decided to get down on his belly and start digging with his hands. As he started scraping away the soil, he caught a glimpse of gold down in that two foot hole.

As he removed more earth, the gold piece kept getting bigger and bigger. It took him over a half an hour to remove this huge piece of jewelry. This was no little trinket. It was a huge torc that weighed 1.5 pounds or 700 grams. It was 7 inches or 20 centimeters in diameter. Could you imagine pulling this thing out of the ground.

The craftsmanship on this piece of jewelry is simply amazing. The end pieces are covered in floral and point work designs, and the center piece is made from eight thin rope like pieces that were twisted together. The entire torc is made from a material called electrum. Electrum is a natural mixture of gold, silver and copper. It was used to make some of the first coins known to man.

Maurice was so nervous about his find that he hid it under

his floorboards until he could get it to the authorities. Upon arriving at the local authorities, Maurice set his find on the table. The first words spoken in the room were, "My God! Where did you get that?"

The torc was in such good condition that the officials told Maurice that it could not possibly be real. It had to be a fake and it was buried in that field as some sort of cruel prank, but they were wrong. The impressive torc was real and it sold for a nice sum of £350,000 or $587,860.

The torc is over 2000 years old and it would have been worn by the most powerful men and women of ancient times. Maurice was well rewarded for his years of metal detecting with this one amazing find. The torc is now owned by Newark's Millgate Museum.

The Crosby Garrett Helmet

Image courtesy of Portable Antiquities Scheme from London, England

The Crosby Garrett Helmet

There are a few items on my "must find" treasure list that still remain "not found." One of them is an ancient sword. I thought I found one of these once, but it turned out to be nothing more than an old car jack. Oh well. It was still fun to dig. The other would be an ancient helmet like the Crosby Garret Helmet.

There is some controversy surrounding this incredible find. The helmet was not determined to be "treasure" by the authorities because it was not made from a precious metal like silver or gold. Because it was not determined to be "treasure," the helmet was allowed to be sold and handled privately. In other words, archeologists were not allowed to look, touch and analyze the piece.

When the helmet was found, it did not resemble what it looks like today. It was found in over 67 pieces in May of 2010 by an anonymous group of metal detecting enthusiasts. The 67 pieces were reconstructed behind close doors by a private party. Archeologists were not allowed to see the pieces before they were put back together.

The archeologist community has expressed outrage at the way this piece was handled and recorded and some of them say that its original find location of Crosby Garrett, Cumbria, England was a complete hoax.

Unfortunately, we may never know the true story of what lies behind this mask.

The Crosby Garrett Helmet

Because it was not declared "treasure," the mask was also allowed to be sold at private auction. This meant that the mask could be purchased by anyone who had the money. It could end up in a private collection behind closed doors. The local Tullie House Museum raised £1.7 million or $2.8 million for the auction. This would not be enough to secure the mask and keep it in its homeland.

The mask was purchased by a private bidder for £2,281,250 or $3,629,469. For something that was not declared treasure, this find sure did sell for a lot of money!

In 2012, the anonymous owner of the helmet decided to let the world see this incredible find. It has been on display at the Tullie House Museum and it has also been on display at the British Museum as well. A truly incredible metal detecting find.

One Final Story

I will leave you with one more story that I think is pretty incredible. This is another personal story of mine from my book: <u>Metal Detecting the Beach.</u>

One summer afternoon I was hunting a stretch of beach that I was very familiar with. The breeze was fresh and beautiful. It was a great day to be out there.

About half way into my hunt, I find a nice crucifix. I wipe the sand from the cross and toss it into my pocket. I was working a good area that was loaded with small change.

The path that I was taking was right towards two women that were enjoying the summer breeze. They were sitting in beach chairs, and each woman had their purse sitting at their feet.

One of the woman looked at me and said, "Finding any treasure?" I nodded and kept on going. The other woman got out of her chair and approached me. This is not unusual. I often get approached by people that are curious about metal detecting. I took off my headphones as she approached.

She looked at me and asked, "Do you ever find anything really good?" "Sometimes." I said.

One Final Story

She asked me if I found anything good today. Usually when someone asks me this, I just say no, but for some reason I felt I should show her the crucifix I found.

I said, "I did find something pretty interesting." I was looking for the crucifix in my pocket. I fumbled with some coins, and then I located the crucifix and pulled it out.

I said, "I found this nice looking crucifix right back there." I pointed in the direction I had just come from.

The woman's face changed, and she turned and walked back to her chair. She started looking through her purse. She came back to me and said, "Can I see that." I handed her the crucifix, and she started to cry.

Now I was in what I would call a very awkward situation. The woman looked me in the face and then she wrapped her arms around me and started hugging me. Her friend approached us and said, "What is going on?"

The woman hugging me exclaimed, "He found my cross. I did not even know it was gone. We were just down there 20 minutes ago and a wave came in with the tide. It knocked my bag over. My crucifix must have fallen out." She started to cry again.

Her friend looked at me and said, "You don't know how important that crucifix is to her. Her mother gave it to her right before she died. She takes it with her everywhere she

One Final Story

goes."

I didn't know what to say or do, so I just kind of stood there for a moment. The woman stopped crying, hugged me again and said, "Thank you!"

I went on my way. I never found anything else that day, but that was an incredible experience!

It's REAL!

It is hard to imagine just how much treasure is hiding right beneath the surface of the earth. The previous finds in this book barely scratch the surface of what is out there. I have personally found thousands of coins, artifacts and pieces of jewelry. I am not bragging. I am simply trying to put things into perspective.

My treasure finds have come from less than 1% of our planet's surface. There must be billions upon billions of lost coins, hoards, caches, jewelry and artifacts buried right under the surface of the earth. Think about that for a minute. Let it soak in.

The reality is this. There is a ton of treasure out there. It could be a penny, or it could be a gold nugget as big as your head. So I leave you with one simple question. What are you waiting for?

Thanks!

Thanks for purchasing my book. If you enjoyed Incredible Metal Detecting Discoveries, then leave a review! I would really appreciate it.

If you are ready to claim your own share of buried treasure, then I highly suggest you read my best selling book entitled:

<u>Metal Detecting: A Beginner's Guide to Mastering the Greatest Hobby In the World.</u>

It is loaded with invaluable information that will help you find your first piece of long lost treasure. Over 200 pages of facts, tips and illustrations. It is available in both digital and print.

If you want to learn what it is like to metal detect at the beach and uncover loads of treasure, take a look at my best selling book entitled:

<u>Metal Detecting the Beach</u>

It is packed full of great beach hunting tips, tricks and secrets. It is available in digital format and paperback.

I am currently in the process of writing several more great

Thanks!

treasure hunting books. If you want to be the first to find out about any new books that I publish, sign up to my **new book release** email list.

I promise not to share your email address with anyone, and I won't send you tons of junk mail. (I will only contact you when a new book is out.) You can sign up at the web address below:

http://eepurl.com/EyhF1

Drop me a line and let me know how you are doing out there. I always love hearing about things that other people are finding. You can email me at:
wordsaremything@gmail.com

Happy hunting,
Mark Smith